MORE PRAISE FOR
DON'T JUST DO SOMETHING, STAND THERE!

"Don't Just Do Something, Stand There! is an exceptional resource that renews one's faith in the utility of meetings and the positive power of effective groups. The book draws on the authors' rich experience to provide practical principles for both seasoned and novice meeting leaders. If you are in search of an approach that is task-focused, makes full use of everyone's experience and expertise, and generates collaborative actions that people will be inspired to implement, this book is for you."

—Joanne Burke, Coordinator, UN Capacity for Disaster
　Risk Reduction Initiative (CADRI), UNDP/BCPR

"Gaining agreement on values and goals among members of our worldwide organization is critical to our continued success. Weisbord and Janoff's skillful facilitation helped us achieve a level of common understanding in three days that otherwise could have taken us years."

—Dick Haworth, Chairman of the Board, Haworth, Inc.

"Weisbord and Janoff's exemplary principles for facilitating group process have helped us create the space where individuals can take responsibility for their learning and act upon the decisions they make."

—Deborah B. Reeve, EdD, Deputy Executive Director,
　National Association of Elementary School Principals

"I have worked with Weisbord and Janoff's principles as Secretary of Corrections in Nebraska and in Washington State. They helped us establish a direction that staff could embrace and rally behind. They facilitated our very diverse perspectives and enabled both agencies to develop vision points that have guided us well into the future."

—Harold W. Clarke, Secretary,
　Washington Department of Corrections

"Facilitating the training of new student leaders each year, I have replaced traditional leadership lectures with meetings building on the students' dreams and plans. Weisbord and Janoff's principles have given me the hope that I had lost in countless sessions of strategic planning. Now I have a way that to my mind can effectively change our school for the better."

—Pieter Booysen, Principal, Afrikaans High School,
　Randburg, Gauteng, South Africa.

"If only every facilitator wo⌷⌷⌷⌷⌷⌷⌷⌷⌷⌷⌷⌷⌷⌷⌷⌷⌷⌷ p to
attend meetings rather than ⌷⌷⌷⌷⌷⌷⌷⌷⌷⌷⌷

—Judy Schector, Director,
　Developing Leadership I
　A Program of The Rober

"Three years of applying these principles have paid off. We began our initiative as a motley collection of activists. Now, we're a growing community network, producing significant results on sustainability issues."
    —Ralph Copleman, Director, Sustainable Lawrence, NJ

"Applying these principles has greatly influenced my practice with groups—both large and small. In today's world of multiple viewpoints and continuous change, leading meetings this way has been quite liberating. It allows groups to act together on what they care deeply about."
    —John Goss, Cinnabar, Johannesburg, South Africa.

"I learned that I could be a much more effective facilitator if I let the groups do their own work. This meant that I had to change my style, contain the anxiety I felt about them 'not getting where they should be' or 'not doing it right,' and allow groups to self manage."
    —Joy Humphreys, thehumphreysgroup,
    Elsternwick, Victoria, Australia

"I have been practicing the 'stand back' approach ever since I attended your program in Philadelphia. Left to my own devices, I would never have found this option. Now it's a safety net, and I feel able to rely on it."
    —Dick Stockford, Director of Strategic Positioning, Ltd,
    United Kingdom

"I've talked with my Australian friends before writing these words. Marvin and Sandra have touched something profound and authentic in many of us. Somehow the way they 'just stand there' creates a space like no other we've known. With them we have experienced a way of leading that allows for confrontation and safety, and tension and relief. There's no pretence, no hidden agenda, no shred of manipulation; And in their new book they double our good fortune by sharing what they do."
    —Tony Richardson, Councilman, Tasmanian Government

"My first exposure to Marv and Sandra's ten principles was in meetings I led in Inuit communities in the high Arctic—a land of sudden and violent winter storms that obliterate familiar reference points and change landscapes. For the traveler caught in a storm an Inukshuk inspires confidence and shows the way. These principles, like the Inukshuk, will bring a sense of hope for folks trying to find their way through the confusing world of organizational change."
    —Mike Bell, Inukshuk Management Consultants

"The principles in this book are widely applicable to many kinds of meetings, not only in the US, but also around the world. I liken using these principles to a swan! Doing less on the water's surface, and managing its own internal mental processes below the surface."
    —Kazuhiko Nakamura, Associate Professor,
    Nanzan University, Nagoya, Japan

"The special gifts Weisbord and Janoff offer are structures and guidelines that free us to be responsible in creating meetings that matter . . . A refreshing antidote to meetings in which leaders and experts tell us what they want us to know and do."

—Barry Oshry, author of *Seeing Systems:*
   Unlocking the Mysteries of Organizational Life,
   and *Leading Systems: Lessons from the Power Lab*

"When I began to apply these principles, I experienced a substantial shift in my role. The less front and center I became as 'the consultant,' the more effective I became as a 'change agent.' The more I tended the process from a base of core principles, the greater the value my presence offered."

—Shem Cohen, Cohen Consulting,
   Albany, NY

"My author-colleagues have done it again, this time for making meetings of all kinds productive. Recipe? A steady focus on intended OUTCOMES, making sure that all the right people are in the room, on an equal footing, relying on their own experiences. In this framework, leaders stay out of the way as good things emerge, a practice requiring understanding and discipline. This book helps you gain both."

—Rolf Lynton, PhD, long-term consultant to creative
   organizations in South and East Asia; emeritus professor;
   and author of the bestselling *Training for Development*

"Blending the ideas of administration and teaching staff with the ideas of parents, students, and non-teaching staff is a somewhat radical notion in the world of schooling...one whose time has come!"

—Chris Kingsberry, educational consultant,
   Philadelphia, PA

"I am grateful for the profound simplicity of these principles. In every engagement I now ask myself—
   1. Have all of the stakeholders been invited?
   2. Are all of the voices being heard?
   3. Are we working toward the future with an emphasis on
      common ground?
   4. Have we considered all the aspects of the situation, including
      the past and the present? And,
   5. What and how much can each participant manage so I can
      get out of the way?"

—Jean Katz, Jean Katz Consulting, Los Angeles, CA

"Marv and Sandra's approach allows for deeper and clearer exploration of differences in a respectful and open manner. However, don't be fooled, it isn't easy. I have experienced the way in which I can change my behavior, my thinking, and my emotional state, to engage with others so we all move forward together."

—Glen Barnes, Director, Breakthrough Consulting P/L, UK

"Over the years I have switched from the expert solving problems to bringing out what people are ready, willing, and able to do. This is a radically different stance. A colleague noticed and said, 'If you are helping them do what they are ready, willing and able to do, how will they know we are providing valuable services?' I replied that our value isn't in what we are doing, but in what the client is doing. That would be all the proof necessary."

—Rick Lent, Brownfield Lent Consulting, Stow, MA

"Valuing structure over controlling behavior is stunning. The seeming simplicity reminds me of a time when I was at Polaroid when we were developing a new state-of-the-art camera. It had only one fastener. All 140 parts snapped together. Some people said that it must be a cheap camera because it only had one screw. Those of us involved realized that it took incredibly creative thinking and technology. Weisbord and Janoff's insights have made something that seems so simple be so elegantly useful."

—Manny Elkind, Mindtech, Inc., Sharon, MA

"Marv and Sandra have taught me to work with group process in a profoundly different way. I've learned how to, 'just stand there' in a way that is productive for the group and not threatening to me. I've learned the extraordinary value of helping groups differentiate AND integrate their perspectives by finding allies in the room; and what I learned about myself in the process has been invaluable."

—Gale S. Wood, COMET Consulting & Coaching, Havertown, PA

"The way of leading meetings has informed our core practices and, even more than that, had reinforced my level of trust in the wisdom of a large and very diverse system."

—Ruth McCambridge, Editor in Chief, The Nonprofit Quarterly

"Marv and Sandra helped us understand that as facilitators we are not there to 'fix' problems. We run the process, the group provides the content and self manages its work. Groups feel safer, enjoy themselves, and are much more productive."

—Bob Campbell and Lynda Jones, Groupwork, Pty Ltd,
    Launceston, Tasmania, Australia

"By the summer of 2000 we knew that without important changes, air traffic, rife with parochialism, would grind to a halt. We chose Marv and Sandra to help us with the challenge. Working with the 'whole system in the room' enabled a significant decision, giving the FAA's Air Traffic Command Center the latitude to put a decades-old practice —'first come, first served'—on the back burner whenever the system was stressed beyond capacity. We made magic in that meeting. This result was previously thought impossible."

—Jack Kies, Metron Aviation, Inc., Former Program Manager for
    Air Traffic Tactical Operations, Federal Aviation Administration

Don't Just Do Something, Stand There!

Don't Just Do Something, Stand There!

Ten Principles for Leading Meetings That Matter

Marvin Weisbord & Sandra Janoff

Illustrations by Jock Macneish

BERRETT-KOEHLER PUBLISHERS, INC.
San Francisco

Berrett-Koehler Publishers, Inc.
235 Montgomery Street, Suite 650
San Francisco, CA 94104-2916
Tel: (415) 288-0260   Fax: (415) 362-2512   www.bkconnection.com

Ordering Information
Quantity sales. Special discounts are available on quantity purchases by corporations, associations, and others. For details, contact the "Special Sales Department" at the Berrett-Koehler address above.
Individual sales. Berrett-Koehler publications are available through most bookstores. They can also be ordered directly from Berrett-Koehler: Tel: (800) 929-2929; Fax: (802) 864-7626; www.bkconnection.com
Orders for college textbook/course adoption use. Please contact Berrett-Koehler: Tel: (800) 929-2929; Fax: (802) 864-7626.
Orders by U.S. trade bookstores and wholesalers. Please contact Ingram Publisher Services, Tel: (800) 509-4887; Fax: (800) 838-1149; E-mail: customer.service@ingrampublisherservices.com; or visit www.ingrampublisherservices.com/Ordering for details about electronic ordering.

Production Management: Michael Bass Associates

Berrett-Koehler and the BK logo are registered trademarks of Berrett-Koehler Publishers, Inc.

Printed in Canada

Berrett-Koehler books are printed on long-lasting acid-free paper. When it is available, we choose paper that has been manufactured by environmentally responsible processes. These may include using trees grown in sustainable forests, incorporating recycled paper, minimizing chlorine in bleaching, or recycling the energy produced at the paper mill.

Library of Congress Cataloging-in-Publication Data

Weisbord, Marvin Ross.
    Don't just do something, stand there!: ten principles for leading
  meetings that matter / Marvin Weisbord and
Sandra Janoff; illustrations by Jock Macneish.
      p.   cm.
    Includes bibliographical references and index.
    ISBN 978-1-57675-425-2 (pbk.: alk. paper)
    1. Business meetings. 2. Meetings. I. Janoff, Sandra, 1945— II. Title.
  HF5734.5.W447 2007
  658.4'56—dc22
                                                                2007014512

First Edition
12 11 10 09 08 07   10 9 8 7 6 5 4 3 2 1

To anybody who ever said,
"Oh, no, not another meeting."

CONTENTS

Preface

This is no ordinary meeting book. Our purpose is to help you improve your leadership skills one meeting at a time. We intend to do that by turning upside down much of the popular wisdom about meeting management. We aim to help you free yourself from the burden of having all the answers to the mysteries of human interaction.

We will introduce you to a philosophy, a theory, and a practice that is at once radical and simple. To apply our ideas you will not need to worry about anybody's behavior but your own. We will illustrate our principles with examples and provide practice tips you can use starting the next time you lead a meeting. We will back up our advice with experiences from colleagues around the world.

Meetings are as common as dirt and about as popular. This presents you with a delicious paradox. You can practice almost any day of the week an art few people trust. You will find that low expectations work in your favor. Every meeting you run gives you a chance to surprise people with a gratifying experience. Why not take it?

Well, you have your reasons. You hate meetings, right? You consider them time wasting, boring, and unproductive, unavoidable rituals to be repeated endlessly in agencies, communities, corporations, and schools. That's just the way things are. Hold on a minute. You may be kidding yourself. While writing this book, we came across research showing no connection between meetings and people's job satisfaction. "It may be socially unacceptable to publicly claim that meetings are desirable," write the researchers. "Instead, a social norm to complain about meetings may exist" (Rogelberg, Leach, Warr, & Burnfield, 2006, p. 95).

Whatever your reality, everybody hates certain meetings for their own reasons. So do we, and we should know. We have been leading meetings separately and together for decades. We have been in more meetings than we can count and taught meeting methods worldwide to thousands of people. We have been burned in meetings that promised much and delivered little; and, alas, we know the guilt of promising more than we have to give. Let us say at the outset that we are not writing about all meetings, certainly not those that rely on speakers, panel discussions, and one-way information. Nor do we deal explicitly with conference calls and online forums, though you may find some of our ideas applicable. Our focus in this book is purposeful, interactive, face-to-face meetings. We present a new way of thinking about and leading gatherings where diverse people solve problems, make decisions, and implement plans. We are writing about meetings where people expect to participate, be heard, and make a difference—in short, meetings that matter. When they are badly led, the main output is cynicism and apathy.

So we write for you if you run meetings. Our book will be of professional interest if you are an executive, manager, consultant, facilitator, or meeting planner. You may also find it useful if you lead work teams, teach school or college, coordinate work in hospitals, chair civic boards, or manage nonprofits.

Our theme is this: you can make every meeting count. You do not have to knock yourself out memorizing checklists to run a good meeting. You can work less hard and get better results. Anytime we "just stand there," we are in no way practicing passivity or indifference. Calm we may be to the naked eye, but a lot is going on inside of us. We stay continuously alert to a few matters—very few, it turns out—that we believe make or break a meeting. Those are the ones we will describe.

In that regard, too, this is no ordinary meeting book. We will not tell you how to interview people or to diagnose a group's needs, before, during, or after a meeting. We will not advise you on how to reduce boredom and apathy, overcome resistance, surface hidden agendas, deal with people who talk too much or too little, or get people's deepest feelings on the table.

To the contrary, we take the position that if you want to accomplish important tasks under trying conditions, you need to work with people the way they are, not as you wish them to be. You do this by learning to manage structure, not behavior. You focus on matching participants to goals, inviting people to share responsibility, and paying attention to the use of space and time. Control a meeting's structure, we will show, and participants will take care of the rest.

This book has been 20 years in the making. Starting in the 1980s, we noted two global trends that made meetings harder to lead. First, we were living in a world changing so fast nobody could keep up. We and many others found ourselves seeking to reduce complexity by ducking it—the "shorter, faster, cheaper" meeting syndrome—and compensating for lack of depth with more entertaining techniques. This proved to be a blind alley.

Second, our meetings grew increasingly multicultural. As businesses went global and nonprofits expanded their reach in health care, education, and sustainability, our participants differed markedly by age, culture, education, jobs, gender, sexual orientation, language, race, ethnicity, and social class. Moving in and out of cultures not our own, we soon learned caution in applying what we took for granted at home. We came upon unspoken cultural norms about which we knew nothing and probably never would. No matter how many theories, strategies, and models we acquired, we had a hard time making our ways of learning fit all the meetings we sought to manage.

We realized that our best methods were no longer producing the desired results. In the late 1980s, we set out to redo from scratch the way we organize, use, and run meetings. First, we vowed to stop wasting people's time. We would no longer attend or lead meetings when we thought the goals were not attainable. Next, we began experimenting with ways to make every meeting matter, even in unfamiliar cultures.

We defined our quest as finding methods anybody could use whether trained or not, whether systems thinkers or not, whether blessed with new technology or not. We set our sights on enabling any group, regardless of culture, education, or language skills to go right to work without having to learn new concepts. We began to structure meetings so that people could cooperate relying only on their own experience.

To make ourselves both more peripheral and more effective, we found we had to make big internal shifts. We had to manage the anxiety we felt as we waited for people to connect across boundaries that no one can simplify. We had to let go of leadership demands on ourselves that we knew to be unrealistic. Rather than worry about outcomes, we taught ourselves to tolerate multiple realities and stay focused on goals.

TEN PRINCIPLES THAT MATTER

The purpose of this book is to introduce you to 10 principles we have evolved for making every meeting matter. They reflect a good bit of refining that we have done on our methods. More to the point, they reflect persistent work on us. Despite recurrent bouts of self-doubt, we have let go of many theories and techniques we once relied on. How, for example, would you diagnose "group needs" when every person needs something different? We could no longer work successfully with increasingly diverse groups in a world of nonstop change using methods favoring homogeneity in more stable times.

In this regard, too, we depart from mainstream meeting guides. To deal with diversity and uncertainty, we offer a single theory that you can use whether looking at organizations, groups, or yourself. It is a theory that we have tested in many cultures. We describe it in the introduction. If you hate theory, skip that part. Stay aware, though, that we ground our practical tips and techniques in research and theory going back decades.

In bringing each principle to life, we have chosen to limit ourselves to a few practices that you can use all the time. We run meetings the same way with teens and senior citizens, students and teachers, artists and engineers, tribal chiefs and captains of industry, making only small adjustments that help people preserve norms central to their identity. We have learned to help people cooperate regardless of their differences by discovering capabilities they did not know they had.

From this book, you will learn to

- help groups achieve shared goals in a timely way,

- manage differences without flying apart,

- solve problems and make tough decisions without delegating the task back to you, and

- structure meetings to greatly increase the probability that people will share responsibility.

While we believe that the action steps we propose are simple to execute, they take self-discipline to learn. You may have to exercise uncommon restraint to "just stand there" when a group falls into chaos and blames it on you; or when somebody says something divisive and everybody looks to you to fix it; or when people split over goals, question your authority, or stereotype each other to the point where work halts. You can, however, learn to deal skillfully with the unexpected if you are willing to persist in working on yourself.

Ours surely are not the only principles and methods for leading meetings that matter. We ask you to consider each one because so many others have adopted them. In writing this book, we compiled stories from colleagues around the world. Hundreds have applied the practices described here in Africa, Asia, Australia, Europe, India, and North and South America. They have integrated our principles into their work regardless of the size, length, and goals of their meetings. You can do the same.

As a fringe benefit, you may lift from your shoulders the yoke of worries about people's attitudes, motives, hidden agendas, status, and styles. Instead, you will learn to use structural practices that keep groups whole, open, and task focused. As you discern when to act and when to just stand there, you will find yourself adding your own positive ripples to the stream of life. In other words, you will learn how to make every meeting matter.

The stone landmark that appears on the cover symbolizes our title. The Inuit of the high Arctic call it an Inuksuk. For centuries they have used it for guidance in navigating the barren tundra. Signifying safety, hope, and friendship, the Inuksuk stands immobile. Yet people rely on it to find their way.

Marvin Weisbord and Sandra Janoff
Wynnewood, PA
March 2007

Acknowledgments

So many people have influenced us, we don't have room to name all of them. In the introduction we cite friends and mentors whose concepts and methods we learned through direct collaboration.

In addition, many colleagues offered us their experiences and comments, expanding our knowledge and enriching the text: Billie Alban, Richard Aronson, Tova Auerbach, Dick Axelrod, Anne Badillo, Jean-Pierre Beaulieu, Susan Berg, Lisa Beutler, Drusilla Copeland, Ralph Copeland, Keith Cox, Shem Cohen, Avner Hamarati, Liisa Hardaloupas, Steve Johnson, Jean Katz, Bengt Lindstrom, Joe Matthews, Phil Mix, Kazuhiro Nakamura, Peter Norlin, Bonnie Olson, Larry Porter, Grace Potts, Judy Schector, Mark Smith, Bill Wood, and Bob Woodruff.

We thank the capable Berrett-Koehler staff who stayed with us through numerous decisions large and small, and in particular Steve Piersanti, who suggested the structure that enabled us to integrate disparate concepts into a single short work. Our diligent reviewers—Steve Cady, Larry Dressler, Sara Jane Hope, and Irene Sitbon—made many suggestions for improving the clarity and accuracy of the text. We also thank several informal reviewers who gave us useful feedback—Claudia Chowaniec, John Evans, Tony Morrison, Douglas O'Loughlin, and Gail Scott. Please attribute any speed bumps that remain to us.

We consider ourselves fortunate to have the fantasy illustrations of our insightful colleague Jock Macneish to enliven the text. As always, we are grateful for support from hundreds of members of Future Search Network. They have confirmed the validity of these principles around the world and made a difference in tens of thousands of lives. Finally, without the love and patience of our spouses Dorothy Barclay Weisbord and Allan Kobernick, and our families, we could not do this work at all.

Introduction:
Making Every Meeting Matter

I want to see progress . . . or it is a waste of time. But that isn't the meeting's fault. That is the fault of the person calling and leading the meeting.

—Darin Hamer, IT professional, Topeka, Kansas (2006)

Our purpose in writing this book is to help you become more effective in the world through the meetings you lead. You will have a chance to master a few simple practices to enhance whatever works for you now. You will learn to recognize procedures that no longer get results. Above all, you will come face to face with the assumptions you make about meetings. If you are going through the motions anyway, why perpetuate cynicism when you can succeed every time?

If you adopt our principles, you will become fanatical about make-or-break matters like matching participants to purposes; and you will manage the daylights out of mundane matters like time frames, rooms, and seating. You also will develop a new awareness of key factors few people notice. You'll pay more attention, for example, to the emergence of informal subgroups that can derail your meeting in an eye blink. You'll become more aware of what people expect from leaders and of the demands you make on yourself.

What you will *not* do is fret over people's motives, attitudes, and personal quirks. In other words, instead of managing other people's behavior, you will manage structure—the conditions under which people interact. The only individual you will seek to manage is you.

We began switching our focus from behavior to structure many years ago. Early in our careers, we noticed some recurring patterns that defeated our aspirations for engagement, outcomes, and follow-up. We found, for example, that the "wrong people" often were in the room. Among them they lacked the expertise, authority, or information to act. That's a structural phenomenon certain to alienate even those with the best intentions. People grew sick and tired of adding more meetings to their calendars. For those who had to show up anyway, we turned ourselves inside out dealing with skepticism at the expense of action. We found it easy to diagnose bad behavior. While diagnosis brings with it the heady illusion of control, most people can't be fixed, no matter how many prescriptions you write. People did, however, fix themselves when we changed the conditions under which they interacted.

We believe that structure becomes more critical the greater the range of differences in the room. If you treat differences as a problem crying for resolution, you undertake an anxious hunt for an elusive quarry. Differences—few of us like them—often divert people from doing their best. Think of difference as a fact of life you can learn to live with. Think of structure as a menu of choices you have for providing people opportunities to take responsibility.

In managing diverse groups, we realized as we crossed cultural boundaries that we could no longer diagnose individual or group needs. We had to learn how to honor differences while building on what people have in common, in particular—the indisputable validity (for every person) of their own experience.

Paradoxically, when you emphasize structure rather than behavior, you may be at your best in situations you once dreaded. You will come to see different worldviews, assumptions, and stereotypes as normal. Perhaps the most liberating discovery we have made is how to enhance a diverse group's capability for action by accepting rather than fixing anybody's shortcomings. If you train yourself to work with people the way they are, you will free yourself from endless suffering.

You will become more effective in two ways.

- First, you will pay more attention to organizing meetings based on purposes. You will discover the increased capability of those involved to reach goals they once thought unreachable.

- Second, you will develop keener instincts for when you need to shift structure and when you don't. As your capability grows for letting people find their own voices, so will your self-confidence in handling new situations no matter what a group chooses to do.

HOW WE CAME TO WRITE THIS BOOK

When a cat chases its tail, success always hurts more than failure. Early in our careers each of us acquired a repertoire essential to our work—for goal setting, team building, problem solving, visioning, strategic planning, conflict management, and self-awareness. We had the unusual privilege of working with many pioneers of group effectiveness. They created a rich storehouse of methods that influenced generations of practitioners.

A Legacy—Ours and Yours

We trace our influences back to the first study ever to document the notable differences among democratic, autocratic, and laissez-faire leaders (Lewin, Lippitt, & White, 1939). This research with young boys doing arts and crafts projects opened up a new vista for action that came to be called "group dynamics."

The practices we advocate were inspired by Ronald Lippitt and Eric Trist, among the founders, respectively, of National Training Laboratories (NTL Institute) in the United States and The Tavistock Institute of Human Relations in Great Britain, and their collaborators Eva Schindler-Rainman and Fred Emery; John Weir (1975) and Joyce Weir, pioneers of personal growth laboratories in "Self-Differentiation"; Yvonne Agazarian (1997), developer of a "Theory of Living Human Systems" of functional subgrouping; Claes Janssen (2005), creator of the "four-room apartment" model of personal and group development; Paul Lawrence, who with Jay Lorsch (Lawrence & Lorsch, 1967) showed how differentiation/integration theory applies to organizations; and the late Gunnar Hjelholt (Madsen & Willert, 2006), a Danish social scientist who inspired us to connect meetings to larger purposes that help people transcend their differences.

To this wonderful legacy we quickly appended more techniques and variations like a cat spinning ever-faster toward its elusive goal. As the world grew more diverse and the pace of change went ballistic, we lined our bookshelves with more methods than we could use in two lifetimes. We were managing our own anxiety by creating higher hurdles, believing that the bigger the tool kit, the better carpenters we would be. By the late 1980s, we realized we would never have at our fingertips the right procedure for all the variations on culture and personal style that we ran into. Nobody could devise all-purpose hammers fast enough to bang away at the emerging multiple dilemmas of escalating complexity. The only way to exit this obstacle course was to stop chasing techniques.

RETHINKING EVERYTHING

Thus, we began a transition that took some years. We decided that if the goals were too big for the people, we would not run the meeting. We began turning down requests to squeeze a day's worth of work into 2 hours. We pared down our repertoire to a few structural procedures nearly anybody could follow. We determined to manage meetings in such a way that people could use the experience, skills, and aspirations they already had. Thus, action would be inevitable unless people consciously chose not to act. We adopted a theory about when to jump in and when to just stand there. We committed to a philosophy based on accepting people as we found them, not as we wished them to be.

Along the way, we poured our early experiences into a strategic planning book we called *Future Search* (Weisbord & Janoff, 2000). There we told how we dropped one by one most of the meeting procedures we once relied on. Some of our changes were heretical. We did away with hallowed concepts like conflict management and priority setting. For these we substituted common ground (agreement by all) and voting-with-your-feet (setting priorities based on willing actors rather than good ideas). We focused on dialogue—having all views heard without needing to act on them. We became alert to those moments when people might scape-goat one another with careless comments, diverting every-body from the task.

We dropped labels like "resistance" and "defensiveness," choosing instead to see people doing their best with what they had. We stopped listing problems as the first step, building instead toward a comprehensive picture of the whole and a preferred future before deciding what needed to be done. We stopped asking what went wrong and how to fix it. Instead, we substituted "What are the possibilities here, and who cares?"

Managing large groups of dozens or hundreds, we made our unit of change the capacity of the whole for action, not the satisfaction of each person's needs or the perfection of every small group's process skills. We encouraged breakout groups to self-manage, precluding the need to have them led by expert facilitators. We stopped assuming that people who said nothing supported the goals and decisions. We paid the most attention to those critical moments when groups were at risk of fragmenting, fighting, or running away.

Under these conditions, people got more done in less time and with greater satisfaction than they ever did when we tried to manage all the details ourselves. The less we did, the more others took over. They did not need to be coaxed into action or provided with complex follow-up strategies. We never tried to change anybody. What we changed were the conditions under which people met. To our surprise, the more we practiced structural change, the better people managed their relationships. Changing a meeting's structure, we found, was the shortcut for people wanting to change their own behavior.

LEARNING TO STAND THERE

Most of all, we changed ourselves. We let go needing to have all the answers, figure out each group's problems and blockages, and keep everybody happy all the time. We taught ourselves to act less and pay attention more. Ours became an alert form of "just standing there," observing, listening, and inviting people to say what was on their minds without prompting them to be positive, negative, or any way except the way they chose to be.

Recently our friend Dawn Rieken gave us a wonderful description of this way of being—quiet on the outside, active inside. Active on the inside is what we are most of the time. The trick is to change the inner dialogue from anxiety to observing without having to fix everything. Instead, we rely on a theory about what it takes for people to manage themselves. Our theory, which we will get to in a moment, is our security blanket.

There are times, however, when people want to fight or flee the goals, the task, the problem, or decision. At those moments we become visibly active. We move in, saying and doing the least that will interrupt a potential fight, clarify an elusive goal, or pose a choice. In those moments, we learned, we are at our best when we can contain our own anxiety and quiet ourselves inside.

In short, when people work the task, we do nothing overt. When they put themselves at risk of fighting or running away, we calm ourselves and become as active as we need to be to get the meeting back on track.

DISCOVERING DIFFERENTIATION/ INTEGRATION THEORY

Early in our collaboration, we had a rewarding "aha" that made possible this book. Each of us, Sandra in education and psychology, Marv in business and organizational consulting, had relied on versions of the same structural theory. We both were applying differentiation/integration (D/I) theory to our work with students, clients, and even ourselves.

This is not to say that we had the legendary "all-purpose hammer." A theory is not a method. It's a way of interpreting reality that helps you act with more certainty. D/I theory helped us make sense of puzzling complexities in a world of increasing diversity, multiple agendas, and nonstop change. For what we aspired to do, that was quite enough.

D/I Defined

Noah Webster's big dictionary says that differentiating means "to distinguish and classify"—that is, to group similar things together. It also can mean to "isolate, ostracize and segregate." Likewise, integrating has two faces. In a positive sense, it means "to make one or harmonize"; in the negative, "to centralize and orchestrate."

To become better meeting leaders, we decided our challenge was to help people differentiate their stakes without excluding anybody and integrate their goals without our forcing unity. Moreover, we came to understand that unless people differentiate their stakes, they are unlikely to act together. Wanting harmony, wholeness, cooperation, and shared goals, we had to start by validating differences. Seeking integrated action, we could not avoid polarities. We had to learn to make them legitimate.

Key D/I Principles

D/I theory has a long history in biology, mathematics, social psychology, and developmental psychology. To begin at the beginning, D/I applies to your earliest moments on Earth. You started life as a single cell that divided and subdivided. Your cells evolved to perform different functions—a beating heart, a thinking brain, a digestive system, each unique in purpose and structure, integrated into a one-of-a-kind working model of a human being.

The organizational analogies should be obvious. Imagine a company that exists to deliver any product or service. Its functions could include research and development, manufacturing, sales, and information systems. They are differentiated, each with its own structural needs. None can accomplish the mission alone. They are faced with a tricky D/I task: holding onto their differences *and* integrating toward a result bigger than any of them. They cannot afford to act in ways that deny the necessity of each.

Our job as leaders/managers/facilitators is to set things up so that people can accept their differences and integrate their capabilities for the good of all. Making the leap from "D" to "I" is at the core of effective meeting management.

Many Practical Uses

In this book, we show you some of the many practical applications of D/I theory that we have made. You can use it to understand why some systems function better than others. You can use it when you plan a meeting, figuring out who to invite and how to use "breakout" groups. From D/I theory, you can derive practical procedures for handling conflict, reaching decisions, and implementing action plans. The first time you apply it, you may come to appreciate key meeting dynamics that were not on your radar screen. You will learn more about when to keep quiet, when to speak, and what to say. You'll be able to prove to yourself that a few simple actions can keep groups working in the face of inevitable differences.

Nor is this all. From D/I theory, you will gain insight into your own potential for personal growth. You will learn to use it as a lens for your own projections, helping you contain your anxiety in new situations. You will be in a better position to avoid exchanges that "hook" you into responding in ways you later regret. In short, D/I theory will help you gain a new measure of influence over any system. We intend to make the journey easy and illuminating for you.

HOW THE BOOK IS ORGANIZED

This book has two parts, "Leading Meetings" and "Managing Yourself." In each chapter, we show you the D/I rationale, give examples of effective action, and suggest things for you to try and pitfalls to avoid.

Part One, "Leading Meetings," covers six principles. "Get the Whole System in the Room" (Principle 1) may change forever the way you organize meetings when fast, committed action is called for. Here we show you how to put those with authority, resources, expertise, information, and need in the same conversation. Whether they act or not, they cannot avoid responsibility.

"Control What You Can, Let Go What You Can't" (Principle 2) offers guidance on how you can optimize output by managing a meeting's boundaries—its purposes, time frames, meeting conditions, list of invitees, working group size, shifting coalitions, agenda, and spectrum of views.

"Explore the 'Whole Elephant'" (Principle 3) can save you endless time and the misunderstandings that occur when people leap into problem solving and talk past one another. We show you ways to look at all aspects of a situation before acting on any one part.

"Let People Be Responsible" (Principle 4) provides you with a key philosophical perspective that will help you manage meetings without feeling the pressure to diagnose group norms or to "pysch out" people's motives as a condition for building commitment.

"Find Common Ground" (Principle 5) offers advice on helping people discover values, ideals, and purposes shared by everyone present regardless of differences. We suggest a new approach to problems and conflicts when common ground is your goal. We treat them as information rather than action items, getting them into the open, validating them, and moving on without resolving them.

"Master the Art of Subgrouping" (Principle 6) will put into your hands a little-known structural method that keeps groups whole, on task, and open to new ideas. You will learn to tell the difference between functional subgroups and those based on stereotypes and how to use informal subgroups to head off conflict.

Part Two, "Managing Yourself," contains four principles to help you make yourself a better leader. We write about the benefits of mastering them and some ways to practice the new behavior implied by "just standing there."

"Make Friends with Anxiety" (Principle 7) redefines an unpleasant dynamic as "blocked excitement." You will learn the benefits and procedures for containing anxiety in yourself and in a group, turning it to creative action.

"Get Used to Projections" (Principle 8) presents a practical, albeit unusual, program for managing yourself. We will help you accept your "projections," the loved and hated parts of yourself that you find reflected in other people. The more parts you know, the greater the variety of human beings you can work with. This is a key step to not "taking it personally," that facile advice we give ourselves, often to no avail. We will show you how to use this awareness to ease your path when working with diverse groups whose members are projecting onto you and each other.

"Be a Dependable Authority" (Principle 9) differentiates the authority that leadership confers from authoritarian behavior. One pitfall we will help you avoid is responding inappropriately when other people project their concerns onto you, making you the (unwitting) stand-in for parents, teachers, bosses, siblings, and others they may have once idolized or loathed.

"Learn to Say No If You Want Yes to Mean Something" (Principle 10) provides support for a vastly underrated skill—saying no to unrealistic requests and expectations for "outcomes" and "deliverables" any time you suspect them to be unreachable.

In the conclusion, "Changing the World One Meeting at a Time," we summarize some of the benefits of the philosophy, theory, and practices we have presented. Also included is a bibliography of all referenced authors.

PART ONE

Leading Meetings

Get the Whole System in the Room

Control What You Can, Let Go What You Can't

Explore the "Whole Elephant"

Let People Be Responsible

Find Common Ground

Master the Art of Subgrouping

These chapters present our views on how to plan, organize, structure, lead, manage, and facilitate meetings. Whether you assume responsibility for a meeting's content, its agenda, its processes, and/or its results, you may find some useful tips and traps. We believe that most of our ideas are applicable whether you have formal authority or not.

Please notice that we use the generic term *leading* to cover *all* possible roles you might assume. Anytime you convene a group, or stand up in front and direct the proceedings, or take over briefly to make a presentation, or facilitate a conversation, you are *leading*, regardless of your relationship to the participants, position in the hierarchy, or role in society. You still have choices to make. These include

- whether you think the goal is reachable given the people in the room (Principle 1);

- figuring out what aspects you can influence and which ones you can't (Principle 2);

- how to bring into the conversation all relevant information so that opinions can be formed, problems solved, or decisions made in a way that will satisfy the situation (Principle 3);

- the extent to which you are willing and able to share responsibility with others who also have a stake in what happens (Principle 4);

- whether or not finding common ground will be a useful precursor to future action (Principle 5); and

- how and when to pay attention to subgroups so as to keep people working on the task (Principle 6).

Get the Whole System in the Room

At a meeting a few years back, we presented a case study of IKEA, the global furniture retailer, where 53 people had in 3 days decentralized a global system for product design, manufacture, and distribution (Weisbord & Janoff, 2005). The plan was developed by people from 10 countries and from all affected functions. Customers and suppliers participated, as did the CEO, who signed off on it immediately. The group formed implementation task forces on the spot. Two years later, the business area manager for seating reported that IKEA had transformed its product strategy and now routinely brought product developers, suppliers, and customers together early in the process.

At the end of our talk, one consultant, minimizing this significant achievement, called out, "Well, of course you were able to do all that in 3 days. Look who you had in the room!"

Well, she had a good point, and that is the theme of our first chapter.

Since Marv first proposed "the whole system in the room" as a key step for fast action in 21st-century organizations, this principle has influenced meetings all over the world (Weisbord, 1987, 2004). He derived this idea from studying his own consulting projects over many decades, noting the shortcomings of both expert and participative problem solving as the pace of change accelerated. Many methods that once worked now seemed to lag people's growing aspirations for both systemic (rather than single-problem) solutions *and* for greater inclusion of people in using what they knew (in addition to expert input). Marv concluded that "getting everybody improving whole systems" was the great challenge for a new century. We needed to find methods enabling *everybody* to improve their own systems without having to become systems experts themselves. Experimenting with simple ways to do that, we and many others noticed that including all the relevant people in each meeting produced faster action on problems, decisions, policies, and plans than any other strategy. Moreover, this principle led to greater personal responsibility at all levels. If the participants didn't act, they had only themselves to blame. Whatever meeting methods they used were secondary.

In this chapter, we give you a simple way to think about a "whole system" for any task and suggest how to match the people to the task. Our goal is to enlarge your thinking about what's possible. We want you to consider the idea that no task is too complex *if* the right people can be brought in on it. This will be true for long meetings or short ones. There are literally thousands of meetings held each day in which people, lacking key participants, cannot use their skills, experience, or motivation. Your meetings need not be among them.

While writing this chapter, we asked several colleagues how they had used the whole system principle. The examples described here illustrate the many ways you can define a system and how inviting the right people can lead to extraordinary results.

SIX PRACTICES ESSENTIAL FOR IMPROVING WHOLE SYSTEMS

1. Define the "Whole System"

Define your system in relation to each meeting's purpose. For any issue there will always be a core group supplemented by relevant others. We put "whole system" in quotes because you are unlikely to get every last person. Fortunately, you don't have to. What you need are diverse people who among them have what it takes to act responsibly if they choose.

Think of the right mix as the people who "ARE IN" the room. (A friend pointed out this acronym to us years after we first wrote it on a flipchart, exactly in the sequence you see here! Who says there is no order in the universe?)

We define a whole system as a group that has within in it various people with

Authority to act (e.g., decision-making responsibility in an organization or community);

Resources, such as contacts, time, or money;

Expertise in the issues to be considered;

Information about the topic that no others have; and

Need to be involved because they will be affected by the outcome and can speak to the consequences.

When you define a system to make sure the right people "are in," you enlarge its boundaries. You draw a bigger circle around your community, organization, or topic to include key people who may never have worked together. You offer every person a chance to discover the whole by creating a mosaic from what they already know. You make "systems thinking" experiential rather than conceptual. Indeed, the nature of the whole cannot be understood fully by anyone unless all participate. Nor can people be expected to act responsibly without understanding the impact of what they do. Having a "whole system" in the room opens doors no one has walked through before.

—EXAMPLE—

Influencing a Nation's Conservation Policies

"When I worked in natural resources management for the Southern African Development Community, I arranged many workshops for senior conservation officials," said Steve Johnson of Botswana's Department of Wildlife and National Parks. "Most workshops were week-long and held in a site that represented a natural resources management topic under discussion. After running a number of these, we found that having just conservation officials meant preaching to the converted.

"So I changed course. I invited ministers, permanent secretaries, and directors from other ministries such as finance, commerce and industry, agriculture, tourism, and land affairs, the private sector, tribal chiefs, and other community members. Essentially we got 'the whole system in the room.' Suddenly we had action—to such a degree that a minister from Mozambique proposed a formal Community Based Natural Resources Management Policy in his parliament. The policy was developed the following year. He then asked for a similar workshop for his Mozambican Parliamentary Standing Committee—

a cross-sectional group of parliamentarians—which led to one of the stronger natural resources processes in all of southern Africa."

2. Match the People to the Task

No issue is too large or too small so long as the task is within the capability of those who attend.

—EXAMPLE—
Renewing a Day Care Center

A small district on the north shore of Oahu, Hawaii, involved diverse stakeholders in a planning meeting that would have major impact on local health care, highway safety, the high school curriculum, and many other matters. People became aware, for example, that the community had lost its only day care center for lack of funds, causing a crisis for 30 small children and their families. Two participants, a school cafeteria cook and a retired telephone lineman, inspired by their neighbors' energy, decided to call their own meeting of parents, teachers, and concerned citizens. Within 3 months, after several more sessions, they found new funding and reopened the day care center. Nine years later they had expanded to three centers and were still holding "whole system in the room" meetings to solve problems.

The more far-reaching your objective, the greater your need for a broad selection of diverse players.

—EXAMPLE—
Reducing Gridlock in the Skies

In early 2004, the U.S. Federal Aviation Administration (FAA) faced a terrible prospect: gridlock in the skies by summer unless users of the national airspace could agree on new procedures. For years experts had met to address increasing aerial congestion, only to end with conflict and indecision. This time FAA executives decided on an unprecedented meeting that would include all airspace users—airlines large and small, freight carriers, the military, business and private pilot groups, pilots' and controllers' unions, and others concerned with air traffic. Jaded by years of frustrating encounters, they rehashed stories of the system's growing complexity.

Then a realization dawned on everyone. The relevant players were all present. If this group could not act, no one else would! Vowing at last to "share the pain," they agreed to radical course corrections in the way air traffic is managed. Among other actions, they changed a decades-old norm of assigning airspace priority to aircraft, agreeing that the FAA, the only stakeholder with a systemwide view, would parcel out short delays to multiple flights across the country whenever necessary to minimize long delays at backed-up airports. With everyone present, it took just 18 hours to make badly needed system changes. (Weisbord & Janoff, 2006)

In the preceding example, all the decision makers and implementers shared the problem and its solution. Though they took on a momentous task, they had among them the capability to pull it off. Often, however, the task is too big for the people involved. Perhaps the most common planning error on planet Earth is convening groups to do tasks with key actors missing. This results in a well-known ritual widely reported in the newspapers. A position paper is written. A group of high-level authorities endorse a course of action. Experts agree on what's best for everybody else. Many people assume that if big names or experts bless a plan, anyone who sees it will salute and start implementing. This happens so rarely it's a wonder people waste time and money repeating such folly.

—EXAMPLE—

Experts + Money = 0

A state health agency known to one of our colleagues wished to establish a new policy for addressing teen alcohol and drug use in communities of color. They invited a task force of addiction experts (*Expertise*) and key funders (*Resources*) to study the issue. After deliberating for months, the task force proposed an excellent plan centered on school-based education and a peer-to-peer prevention model. It was promptly undermined by those who were not in the loop—community center service providers (*Information*), administrators and decision makers in education and substance abuse agencies (*Authority*), and teens and families (*Need*). None had been in the planning.

3. Match the Meeting's Length to Its Agenda

Effective whole system meetings do not have to be 3 days in length. You can use short time frames when (a) the agenda is narrowly focused, (b) many others have already spent time working on key issues, and/or (c) the objective is noncontroversial but not well understood. In such cases, what you seek is shared agreement, the next steps people will take, and structures for moving forward.

—EXAMPLE—

Focusing Public Policy on Children's Lives

The Maine Children's Cabinet, five departmental commissioners chaired by the state's first lady, in 2003 identified reducing Adverse Childhood Experiences (ACE) as a top state priority. Maine's Department of Health and Human Services determined to use new research to influence state policymakers and stimulate community action on behalf of children and families. Richard Aronson,

M.D., medical director of Maternal and Child Health, realizing that this ambitious goal required support from
many agencies, organized two intense 2-hour meetings.
Each involved a dozen key people who among them had
what was needed to act but had never met all at once:

- academic experts from the University of New
  England;
- public health nurses;
- representatives of the Women, Infants, and
  Children (WIC) program;
- Child Abuse Action Network workers,
- members of the Child Death and Serious Injury
  Review Panel;
- State Department of Health and Human Services
  staff;
- State Department of Education personnel;
  and
- State Department of Corrections staff.

Sitting in a forum where all views could be heard,
they advanced significantly the joint planning needed to
translate research into public policy. The State Health
and Human Services Department and the University of
New England, for example, agreed to explore a commu-
nity-based research partnership. The meetings also led
to a presentation on the ACE research to the Children's
Cabinet itself, with the strong support of the first lady.
Another outcome was a statewide forum on Adverse
Childhood Experiences and Resiliency, resulting in action that will integrate research into clinical practice.

Aronson has run many such meetings from an hour
to several days using whole system principles. Asked how
he gets so many busy people together at once, he commented, "I've stopped using the word *meeting* because
for so many people, it carries a negative connotation. Instead, I invite people to join a 'dialogue,' 'action-oriented
conversation,' or 'gathering.'"

4. Give People Time to Express Themselves

When the agenda directly affects many people's lives and work, longer meetings become necessary even when the topic is limited to changes in organizational policy and procedure. Whether broad or narrow, when people have strong feelings about what is happening, they need time to come to grips with their feelings before they will "own" the needed action steps.

—EXAMPLE—
Challenging the Status Quo

The Internal Revenue Service (IRS), the national tax collector whose "customers" include every money earner in the United States, had a 15,000-person division dealing with public questions by phone and mail. After an internal merger, executives wanted to foster greater cooperation between headquarters staff and field operations They called a 3-day meeting of 32 key people:

- field operations directors,
- field planning managers who interact with HQ staff,
- HQ senior managers, and
- top executives.

With all key actors involved, the group made immediate changes to its field review processes, installed a new system of weekly voice mails to all managers, set up quarterly staff follow-up meetings across functions, and developed a new reporting structure. What might previously have taken months was implemented in a few days. The meeting was managed by Susan Berg and Mark Smith.

It was not stress-free, said Berg. "We had two highly charged preconference steering committee meetings to identify key issues. We also worked with the director and deputy director in advance to help them get feedback from the steering committee on systemic concerns. Day 1 was tough, as people poured out their feelings about the past, something they needed to do before they could focus on positive experiences. There was a long pause as the group 'stewed' in the mess. Then they made a joint decision to move forward.

"Day 2 was energetic and action oriented. Commented one executive afterward, 'We needed Tuesday to get to Wednesday!' During the meeting, people said that they had never had a real dialogue before, talking openly about what was and wasn't working for them. By day 3, people were in down-and-dirty action planning, talking about what they needed to change."

5. Manage Meetings Using D/I Principles

Three procedures cover most of the situations we encounter.

- To enable *differentiation*, we ask people to speak individually or to work in groups where all share a functional similarity. For example, if the task is strategic planning in a school, we want to hear from teachers, administrators, staff, parents, and pupils, each group clarifying their stakes.

- To help people *integrate* their diverse perspectives, we have people work in mixed groups that cover the spectrum of those present.

- When we use small groups to help people *differentiate* their stakes, we usually engage the whole group in the task of *integrating* what they have learned. We always ask small groups, whether functional or mixed, to report to the whole. When we work with a large group, people often clarify their own ideas and make integrating statements after they have heard reports from all the small groups.

Using these D/I-based practices, we are able to design and manage task-focused meetings for any purpose, so long as we have the right people given the purpose.

—EXAMPLE—
Solving the Hospital Emergency Room Mystery

The head of primary care in a large hospital determined to train medical professionals to become integrative program managers. He organized an experimental workshop for some 20 administrators, clinical pharmacists, nurse-practitioners, and physicians who worked together daily. They had never collaborated in managing their work systems or given it much thought. Each profession had assumptions about its own role and the roles of all the others that none had ever investigated. In short, they often stereotyped one another.

In a key exercise based on D/I principles, the group was given a thinly disguised case known to most, a woman who came into the emergency room with severe dizziness.

The woman told the admitting clerk that she was taking "pressure pills" four times a day. A nurse-practitioner found in the files a prescription written 2 weeks earlier. Except for low blood pressure, the nurse could see nothing wrong. A medical resident agreed. "Just get her to take her pills," said the doctor. "You've got to educate these people." The nurse pointed out that the patient took the pills for months and was fine until now. Then she noted a curious discrepancy. The label on the patient's medicine vial called for a different dosage than what was in the records.

"The pharmacy messed up again!" said the nurse. "I'm calling them."

"Don't bother," said the resident. "They don't listen. Give her a new prescription."

The nurse wrote and the resident signed a new Rx. A few days later the woman came back after a fainting spell. She had with her two bottles of the same medicine under different names. A resident physician called the pharmacist who found two prescriptions written 2 weeks apart, one generic, one brand name. The patient thought she was taking two medicines.

"You should have caught this!" said the resident to the pharmacist. "Don't you talk to your clients?"

The pharmacist said that the woman told him she knew what to do. "This is what happens," he added, "when doctors just countersign Rx's and don't really evaluate a case!"

At that point the screening resident called the clinic resident, and both agreed it was the nurse's fault for not taking the first bottle away from the patient. Said the nurse, "This only happens when physicians sit around in little offices reading journals!"

The case drew rueful smiles. Rather than address their conflicts, we asked people to differentiate into four functional groups—nurse-practitioners, pharmacists, physicians, and administrators. Each group was asked to "diagnose" the situation. How did the patient get into trouble? Each profession had its own point of view, albeit limited.

Next, to integrate their perspectives, we had people reorganize into five cross-disciplinary groups of four persons each. The new groups were asked to make a "responsibility chart" such that this situation could never happen again. To each professional involved in the case, they were asked to agree on one of four designations:

- the letter *A* for "final authority,"

- *R* for "responsibility to act,"

- *S* for "support with resources," and

- *I* for "must be informed before action is taken."

All groups presented creative solutions. A stunned silence followed the last presentation. No two responsibility charts were alike. One of the physicians rose from his chair, clapped a hand to his head, and said, "Can you believe it? There's no right answer to this!"

In fact, there were five "right answers," each an integrated solution agreed to by a group of diverse professionals. The solution lay not in an ideal procedure but rather in everyone understanding one another's experience and deciding together how best to serve the patient. Each professional knew more about the emergency room system by the end of the exercise than any of them knew at the start. The process required about 3 hours.

6. Use the "3 by 3 Rule" If You Can't Get the Whole System

This is not rocket science. Get any three levels and any three functions into the same conversation on any issue of mutual concern. You will gain a better resolution much faster if you provide people firsthand access to the other parts of the systems on whose behavior they rely. The underlying concept is that you can only change a system in relation to the larger system of which it is a part. That is why "team building" creates better work teams without improving whole companies. Every team meeting gives rise to many more meetings before the work done at the center impacts the whole.

—EXAMPLE—
"Where's Your Boss in All This?"

The management team in a small division of a large company met to improve their effectiveness. Within a few hours, it became plain that their hands were tied for lack of cooperation with the large, centralized corporate quality, finance, and human resource staffs. Each was run by a peer of the division president, and all reported to the big company's COO.

As the frustration built, one manager blurted out to the president, "Where's your boss in all this? He's the only one who can help us." During lunch, the president phoned his boss, who showed up an hour later. He listened for 20 minutes to a litany of annoying practices that defeated his call for close cooperation between staff and line. After a few pointed questions, he excused himself and got on the phone to each of the other departments. When he returned, he said, "I think we're on the right track now." Next day, he convened a meeting of the division and staff executives. After months of frustration, the situation—following a three-level dialogue—was on its way to resolution within 24 hours.

PRINCIPLE 1: In Summary
• •

Define a "whole system" as those who have among them authority, resources, expertise, information, and need. Get the right cross section if you want action on problems and decisions without a lot more meetings.

Suggestions for Your Next Meeting

- Define the whole system in light of your goal. Use the ARE IN checklist. Who has formal authority? Resources? Expertise? Information? Need?

- Match the people to the task. Make a note on your expected outcome. For each of those who ARE IN, note the consequences of leaving them out.

- Match the length to the agenda. How much time do you think you need? Be honest. Be realistic.

- Give people time to express themselves. How will you take advantage of the diverse perspectives in the room? (In future chapters, we present many methods for doing this.)

- Use differentiation and integration in your plan. Think about when to ask people to work alone, in small groups, or in the whole group. Remember that you can't integrate unless people know all the range of possibilities. So get it all out early if you want to make progress.

- Try the "3 by 3 Rule." Pick a problem or decision that involves more than one department or function. Get any two other functions that have a stake and/or three organizational levels, preferably both. Pick a goal that is realistic for the time available.

Control What You Can,
Let Go What You Can't

Quiz for Ourselves

Q: What would you like to control?
A: People's behavior, commitment, motivation, and outcomes.

Q: What can you control?
A: Structure.

Q: Anything else?
A: Our own behavior.

Q: What have you let go of?
A: Controlling others' behavior, commitment, motivation, and outcomes.

Q: Why?
A: We can't do it, and we get better results by not trying.

DISCOVERING SELF-MANAGEMENT

It was the late Eric Trist, a founder of London's Tavistock Institute of Human Relations, who went down into a South Yorkshire coal mine in the late 1940s and came up "a changed man." He had seen a work system until then considered implausible. The miners and management had collaborated to create multiskilled self-managing teams that planned and controlled their own work. The teams had higher output, less downtime, fewer accidents, and less absenteeism than anybody had believed possible. They had read no management books, taken no personality tests, attended no problem-solving courses, and heard no motivational speakers. They invented a highly productive work system using knowledge and experience they already had.

Tens of thousands of others, we among them, have learned from the miners' innovation to work more effectively. We call ourselves "structuralists" because we know from years of trial and error that it is easier to create structures within which people manage their own behavior than it is to make people behave the way we want. Thus we manage group composition, division of labor, time, use of space, goal focus, and subgrouping. Paradoxically, had we not for years studied attitudes, conflict management, diagnosis, meeting dynamics, and motivation, we could not assert now with authority that complex times call for simpler practices.

CONTROLLING WHAT IS CONTROLLABLE

The point of this chapter is as radical as it is simple: you do not need to suffer through futile meetings trying to figure out what is wrong with people and how to fix them. For years we have run large-group planning meetings around the world. If you were to walk in on one of these, you would see several small groups, each with its own chart pad, sitting in a bright, airy room, working intently with high energy on an important task. The groups are managing themselves—keeping time, taking notes, making room for all views, and preparing reports to the whole. They have a task that draws on everyone's skills and experience. The flipcharts could well be in a language that neither you nor we understand. You would have no way of knowing who is leading the meeting.

We are not advocating that all meetings be run like self-managing work teams. Rather, we wish to reinforce the point that most people have a great deal of capability for self-control that meeting leaders rarely take into account. Whatever the circumstances, whatever your goals, you are likely to get better results managing boundaries than trying to make people do what you want.

We've let go believing we can manage what individuals feel, think, say, and do. Our unit of change is not any person or even any small group. Rather, we seek to structure meetings so that all become capable of acting beyond the capacity of any one person. We identify a successful meeting by a group's increased capability to self-manage their own problem solving and decision making. When people do things after a meeting that seemed difficult or impossible beforehand, we feel confirmed in the path we have chosen.

You have the most leverage on a meeting's success before a single person walks into the room. We urge that every time you plan a meeting, you control as many factors as you can. The more you manage the conditions under which people meet, the less you will need to manage their meeting behavior. Fortunately, it is much easier to structure a meeting for success in advance than to worry about the motives and habits of people once they arrive. Here we will suggest what you could seek to control before the meeting, followed by what to control once it starts.

EXERCISE MAXIMUM CONTROL BEFORE THE MEETING

If it's your meeting, don't hold it until you have the conditions right. If you run the meeting for someone else, don't agree to do it unless you believe you will succeed. Here are guidelines to consider.

1. Know Your Role

If you are a group's formal leader, the buck stops with you. You can fall into one of two traps: withholding what you know, hoping others will come around, and/or imposing your ideas without hearing any others. To avoid either extreme, decide before going into the meeting where you stand and how open you are to other ideas. Prepare to say what you know and what you believe; in other words, be a "dependable authority" (Principle 9).

There are other ways to think about your role. Our colleague Larry Porter, veteran of a thousand meetings, created a matrix of leader roles depending on the extent to which you (a) manage the meeting and (b) are involved in the content. He calls it "Facilitator Boundaries," highlighting which aspects of the work are yours and what tasks you leave to others. (Larry maintains boundaries by addressing a group as "you" when he has no content responsibility and/or formal authority, and he uses "us" and "we" when he leads a group to which he belongs or heads.) Here are four possible roles:

		Have You a Stake in the Content?	
		NO	**YES**
Are You Managing the Meeting?	**NO**	Process Only (PO)	Process and Content (PC)
	YES	Process and Meeting Management (PM)	Process, Content, and Meeting Management (PMC)

Process Only (PO)—You have no management or content tasks. Your role is to observe and comment on how the group is doing.

Process and Meeting Management (PM)—You may be employed to manage a meeting without responsibility for its content. Participants provide information, analysis, conclusions, decisions, and action plans. Future Search facilitators and internal consultants typically take this role. The responsibility is for structure rather than content. If you use a particular meeting model, you advocate explicit structures within which to frame goals, time required, room setups, and formal subgroups. However, the content comes entirely from participants.

Process and Content (PC)—This is a typical role for experts hired, for example, to help a group plan a building, raise money, fix an environmental problem, or mount a public health campaign. In this case you have experience with solutions, interact with the group, and deliver your best advice. A person in authority runs the meeting, but you are on stage much of the time; and you will have great influence over goals, time frames, and agenda.

Process, Content, and Meeting Management (PMC)—In this role, usually, but not always, you are a member of the group and may have formal authority, too. In short, you assume a great deal of responsibility for process, content, and, therefore, outcomes.

Larry's advice, seconded by us, is that once you know your role, make it explicit to the others. You don't want people to be surprised when you switch from soliciting ideas to adding your own two cents from the authority chair. This can be tricky, changing roles in midmeeting. The best anybody can do, in our opinion, is to (a) stay aware of your role, (b) tell people your intentions, and (c) let people know when you change hats.

2. Clarify the Purpose—for Yourself

Every meeting has a purpose. Does the purpose make sense to you? What will the output be? Is it achievable in the time you have? Whether you are a formal leader, content expert, or facilitator, you will get more if you know going in what product you want. Whether you plan for 10 people or 1,000, the first question to ask is "Why? What is required here? Information, decisions, solutions, action plans—any or all?" We make it a practice at the start of every meeting to check our understanding of the purpose against that of the participants.

—EXAMPLE—
"Are the Goals Clear?"

During the boss's opening remarks in a multilingual strategic planning meeting, we noticed some people looking blank when asked if the goal was clear to everyone. Rather than repeating what had been said, we asked people to talk in small groups for 5 minutes about what they had heard. We then had the groups ask specific questions. These were answered by appropriate people until everyone was satisfied.

3. Assure That Participants Are Equal to the Task

Get straight in your head that you cannot lead, facilitate, or manage your way out of a meeting when key people are missing. Your leadership style will never carry you that far no matter how much training you have. That is the point of Principle 1. If action is called for, a decision required, a problem to be solved, commitments to be made, you waste everybody's time acting without the actors, decision makers, and problem solvers.

Prior to any meeting, we check to see if the people are equal to the goal. If we control the invitation list, we want a mix of those with authority, expertise, information, resources, and need. If we don't control the list, we check to see that those in charge can get the people needed to do the job. It is our responsibility to know that we can reach the goal in the time available with the people who show up. You need no special training to implement this guideline. Your motivation could be an unquenchable desire to succeed.

—EXAMPLE—
The Lesson We Will Never Forget

Many years ago, adventurous and confident, we were asked to lead merger meetings for two banks' operations departments. Our clients were the respective executive vice presidents. With them we devised a strategy that would start with a joint policy meeting of executive teams followed by meetings of some 1,200 others to plan the implementation. The most contentious issue in the executive meeting was where to locate a merged operations center, 80 percent of the staff, that involved consolidating massive computers. Each bank wanted the center in its home city. The cities were several hundred miles apart.

The group was deadlocked until we proposed that each bank's executives make a case for the *other* city. They separated for an hour, then came together to hear one another's arguments. Within minutes, they agreed that City A was the better choice. "This means I'll have to leave, because I can't relocate my family right now," said one VP. "But I know this is the right thing to do!" After three tough days, we and our clients left the meeting feeling mighty pleased with ourselves. A few days later, we got a call from one of the operations heads. "We told the boss of our decision for City A."

"Wonderful," we said. "What was his response?"

"Well," came the reply, "he lives in City B, and he wants to be close to the action. He said he wasn't moving."

"What will you do?" we asked.

"Dust off my résumé," he said.

4. Use Subgroups to Differentiate and Integrate Views

Once we know a meeting's purpose and time frames, we turn our attention to group size. Most small-group meetings require only one structure, a committee of the whole. If we work only in one group, differentiation occurs as each person speaks or when a show of hands is asked for. There are occasions, though, when we might ask for explicit subgroups—pairs, trios, quartets, eights, and so forth. You can differentiate groups by function, geography, experience, and a host of other criteria. You might do this to

- create differentiated perspectives (e.g., parents, teachers, students, and administrators in a school planning meeting);

- give interest groups a chance to clarify their positions (e.g., when there are various solutions to a given problem);

- organize action groups differentiated by the tasks they undertake (e.g., when people divide complex plans into manageable projects).

Simply asking people to form small groups is *not* what we mean here. If you organize random groups, with no basis in similarities, differences, or preferences, you are not "differentiating." You are just forming small groups. In our framework, we differentiate to integrate. Integration requires that people interact across boundaries of differences made explicit, seeking to build on all their resources and needs.

—EXAMPLE—
Different People, No Differentiation

A long time ago, in the years leading up to Future Search, we managed a meeting to create a technical assistance consortium for manufacturers in a southern state. About 45 people attended, a cross section of key stakeholders with a spectrum of views. We were sure people would educate each other as they worked together. We organized undifferentiated small groups with no reference to function. The groups worked with energy and reported with enthusiasm. What they did not report was a spectrum of the clearly articulated viewpoints that they held. They cooperated, to be sure, at the expense of real integration. By the time it became clear to us that exploring their many perspectives was needed if we were to get innovative plans, time was up. The meeting ended with weak action commitments. This experience confirmed for us that simply having different people working together in a room is not enough.

5. Plan to Have Each Group Report to the Whole

The number of small groups that can meet at once is infinite. If you have people talk in small groups and do nothing with their conversations, you are facilitating parallel meetings. You cannot advance the purposes of the whole unless everyone hears what the small groups have to say. We always plan for small groups to (a) report to each other and (b) talk over, question, or respond to what they hear from other groups. Each step takes time. The larger the group, the more time you need for each activity.

6. Allow Enough Time

Some goals take hours. Others take days. Time is your scarcest resource. When it's gone, it's gone. It's also controllable. Match time to the goals by asking, "What needs to happen for this group to reach its goal? How long must I allocate to each step?" Whether the meeting lasts 3 hours or 3 days, your achievements are bounded by purpose, group size, and time available. Satisfy yourself that you have the three in balance.

If you want an implementable plan, you need to allocate time so that people can

- collect their thoughts,
- differentiate their stakes,

- integrate their ideas, and

- make action commitments.

Ordinarily, all this takes days rather than hours. You may need several shorter meetings stretched over weeks or months.

The more complex the task, the more people you may need. The more controversial the issue, the more time people need to differentiate their stakes. Until they do, they will have a hard time making integrated decisions. If you want content without commitment, you can limit input to experts and top dogs. If you want content with high commitment, don't skimp on time for people to interact with the issues and each other.

7. Choose Healthy Working Conditions

Rooms   This has been our hobbyhorse for years. Choose your meeting room with care. Choose it to support participants' health. Make it easy for people to hear, see, interact, and move around. Life in the 21st century is stressful enough without working in rooms certain to increase tension. Basement dungeon rooms are bad for your mental and physical health. People who embrace a notion that you can do better work in windowless spaces strike us as literally having lost touch with their senses. Not one of the thousands of people we have worked with ever complained they were distracted looking out the window!

When you have a choice opt for spaces with doors that open to outdoor patios or balconies. Give people breaks out of doors when weather and climate permit. Otherwise, set up meals and breaks in other rooms, allowing people a walk and a change of scenery.

Indeed, many people use the environment explicitly to advance a meeting's goals. Larry Dressler, for example, has held strategic planning meetings on the coast, "using the ocean and skyline as a metaphor for different aspects of strategic thinking." Our colleague the late Gunnar Hjel-holt, training a Danish oil tanker crew, ran a weeklong session in an inn adjacent to the shipyard, allowing trainees to visit their new ship as it was being built. When practical, we like to hold Future Search planning meetings in the room we will use, so that we know for sure how the space will work, and our steering committee can visualize what will take place.

—EXAMPLE—

A Blinding Flash of the Oblivious

Insisting on an ideal room, we once arrived at a conference center to find the curtains drawn. A meeting arranger had closed them to "avoid distractions." When we drew back the curtains, we found ourselves looking out on the Pacific Ocean, great foamy waves crashing against the rocks, whales spouting in the distance, palm trees swaying in the wind. The view was spectacular. We assured our worrier that working with the curtains open was a problem we could live with. The huge lightness of spirit you could feel in that room persisted long after people let go the view and got down to work.

Sound Acoustics matter, too. In rooms with bare walls of wood, plastic, or metal and bare wooden floors, sound bounces around like a ball on a squash court. Rooms with too-high ceilings boom with echoes, and people strain to hear each other. We feel fortunate when we can find carpeted rooms and ceilings that absorb sound instead of turning speech into noise. For large-group meetings, we ask for handheld cordless microphones that can be passed around like "talking sticks." Indeed, such mikes offer people wonderful opportunities for self-managing.

Snacks We advocate healthy options for breaks (e.g., fresh fruit and nuts) to go along with the omnipresent pastries and candies. We are not the sugar police. Still, we know we work a lot harder if people only have sweets and no access to protein during afternoon breaks.

Accessibility In many countries, people are required by law to make restrooms and meeting rooms easy to use for those needing wheelchairs or with other disabilities. Required or not, we consider it essential that key spaces be accessible to all participants for the meetings we manage.

Sustainability Finally, meetings mean little if inadvertently we destroy our shrinking planet. In recent years we have become aware of convenient ways to reduce our "footprint" on the Earth. Our colleague Ralph Copleman recommends many things you can control—reusable nametags; notepads and flipcharts made from recycled paper; ceramic coffee mugs; a recycling bin in the room. If you furnish a meeting room, check out "cradle-to-cradle" furniture, the components of which will be reused rather than trashed.

EXERCISE MINIMAL CONTROL DURING THE MEETING

If we lead a meeting, we want people to know at the start what we expect of them and ourselves. We always say what we believe the goal to be and check whether others agree. Often, if the group is large and will be together for more than a day, we propose a working agreement by way of acknowledging the division of labor. The figure that follows shows our generic agreement when managing meetings for others. The proposal would be different if we had formal authority and/or content expertise.

Here are the factors that we attend to once the meeting begins.

1. Watch for Fight or Flight

There are times when people, despite their best intentions, lose sight of the task. They may change the subject, challenge one another, shut up entirely, or vote with their feet and leave the room. If you follow Principles 1 (Whole System in the Room), 3 (Explore the "Whole Elephant"), and 4 (Let People Be Responsible), you will have fewer concerns with these contingencies. When managing large groups, we acknowledge at the start our responsibility for reminding people of the goal and time constraints. We learned years ago that large-group meetings easily become lightning rods for every agenda anybody has ever had. We accept this as natural and rarely need to interrupt the action to keep a meeting on track.

If you do find a group wandering off, here's a suggestion from Jean Katz, a strategic planner who has worked extensively with school boards. Rather than drift along or try to redirect attention, Jean says to the group, "Take a minute to write down exactly what you want at this moment." She then asks people to read what they have written. What happens? "We're able to talk about what the common threads are," she says, "and we find our way back to the goal."

2. Head Off Interactions That Might Alienate or Isolate Someone

During every meeting, we pay attention to subgroup dynamics, acting when it looks like someone might be excluded or when the group has polarized over an issue and may attack some member over a difference. These are among the few times when we actively seek to direct people's attention. We interrupt dysfunctional transactions by surfacing informal subgroups. This topic is covered thoroughly under Principle 5.

3. Arrange Seating to Fit the Purpose

We pay attention to how people are seated. Chairs in rows direct the conversation to the leader. Seated in a circle, people find it easier to interact. Years ago we were forced by circumstance to remove tables from a room too small to hold 60 participants. Our limitation proved a blessing. We realized that the tables were more hindrance than help, especially when people moved in and out of small groups. We learned that group members sitting in circles of six or eight make better contact when they don't have tabletops between them. We also learned that chairs with wheels make it easy for people to organize and reorganize themselves.

4. Establish Time Management Norms Early

We usually tell people that time is our scarcest resource, and we want their help in managing it. We have a technique that makes this point. When we ask people to introduce themselves, we say that we would like to hear from everybody in *X* minutes. We set an outer limit that makes sense given the group size and length of meeting but do not specify how long each person should take.

In meetings of a day or more, we use this go-around to further the group's task, asking people such questions as what they understand the goal to be, why they came, and/or what resources they bring. You will be amazed at how much information 40 or 50 people will share given 25 or 30 minutes. To facilitate self-managing, we ask that a volunteer signal the group every 10 minutes. Some people take more time, some less. Rare is the group that exceeds its allotment. People learn at the start that they can cooperate to use their scarcest resource wisely.

It is easier to end a meeting early than to extend it. Should we schedule an earlier close and negotiate for an extra half hour at day's end, we lose some people and alienate others. If we find ourselves ahead and propose ending early, we get a round of applause.

We also are mindful that some people habitually arrive late and leave early. We cannot let a few people determine the fate of a group. We start with those who come on time. If many people announce in advance that they will be late and/or leave early, we ask group members what they want to do.

We also are aware of cultural time norms. Many times we have managed meetings where we were told, "You have to understand, here we operate on XYZ time. People come late—that's just the way it is." In such places, we recalibrate our expectations. We'd be foolish to pretend we can do 3 hours of work between 9 and noon when half the group won't show up before 10. Every time somebody straggles in, the whole group slows down. And the latecomers have a hard time catching up.

Nevertheless, we always start on time with those who show up. The most practical solution to people coming late we owe to Ronald Lippitt, the co-inventor of "group dynamics" and an ingenious meeting methods innovator. Ron created for early arrivals the "raggedy start," offering something useful for them to do that furthered the meeting's goal. Using this procedure, we have people talk to each other about what they are learning, sort information from the previous meeting, generate questions, or do any task that adds value. As newcomers arrive, they join existing groups or form new ones. When all or most arrive, the group continues as one.

Sometimes small groups ask for more time after using up their allotment. We recall a group of financial staffers who asked for 10 minutes more after everyone else was finishing. "If your group takes 10 minutes here," we said, "we'll have to decide how to make up the time later." Being good with numbers, they said "Got it!" and went back and finished on time.

Managing Breaks   In most of the world, it is customary for people to take breaks morning and afternoon. Rare is the group where every member returns from a break on time. We have found that if we habitually start on time following a break, people are less likely to be late. If lateness becomes an issue, we ring a bell with a minute to go, or ask a group member to call the others in. We also encourage individuals to take personal breaks whenever they wish, without waiting for formal breaks.

Principle 2: In Summary
....

Exercise maximal control before the meeting (e.g., your role, participants, agenda, and time). During the meeting, control only those few things needed to keep people working on the task.

Suggestions for Your Next Meeting

- Know your role. Are you dealing with content, process, or both? How will you describe your role to the group?

- Clarify purposes relative to time. Write down the goal. Can you reach it in the time available?

- Assure participants are equal to the task. Are you satisfied that you can do the task with the people who will attend?

- Arrange seating for the purpose. Next time you find chairs set up in rows, ask people to put themselves in a circle. Or get rid of tables. Note the impact on the meeting.

Explore the "Whole Elephant"

If you're wondering how elephants figure in meetings that matter, let us introduce you to a famous poem by the Vermont lawyer John Godfrey Saxe (1816–1887), who recast in verse an ancient Buddhist teaching. See whether you can identify with it.

The Blind Men and the Elephant

It was six men of Indostan to learning much inclined,
Who went to see the Elephant (though all of them
    were blind),
That each by observation might satisfy his mind.

The First approached the Elephant, and happening
    to fall
Against his broad and sturdy side, at once began to
    bawl:
"God bless me! but the Elephant is very like a wall!"

The Second, feeling of the tusk cried, "Ho! What have
    we here,
So very round and smooth and sharp? To me 'tis
    mighty clear
This wonder of an Elephant is very like a spear!"

The Third approached the animal, and happening
    to take

The squirming trunk within his hands, thus boldly up
    he spake:
"I see," quoth he, "the Elephant is very like a snake!"

The Fourth reached out an eager hand, and felt about
    the knee:
"What most this wondrous beast is like is mighty
    plain," quoth he;
"'Tis clear enough the Elephant is very like a tree!"

The Fifth, who chanced to touch the ear, said: "E'en
    the blindest man
Can tell what this resembles most; deny the fact who
    can,
This marvel of an Elephant is very like a fan!"

The Sixth no sooner had begun about the beast to grope,
Than, seizing on the swinging tail that fell within his
    scope.
"I see," quoth he, "the Elephant is very like a rope!"

And so these men of Indostan disputed loud and long,
Each in his own opinion exceeding stiff and strong,
Though each was partly in the right, and all were in
    the wrong!

Moral: So oft in theologic wars, the disputants, I ween,
Rail on in utter ignorance of what each other mean,
And prate about an Elephant not one of them has seen.

ANCIENT WISDOM MEETS SYSTEMS THINKING

Now, with the "whole system" in the room, let us connect the dots between elephants and meetings. We refer you to biologist Ludwig von Bertalanffy's (1952) world-changing book, *General Systems Theory*. In case you find it hard going, here is our concise summary: Everything is connected to everything else. An elephant consists of all its parts. Nothing can be nurtured and grown in isolation, not individuals, not groups, not organizations or whole nations. This was a relatively new idea in 1960 when the applied social scientists Eric Trist and Fred Emery were invited to conduct a leadership course to accelerate the merger of two British aircraft engine companies (Weisbord et al., 1992).

In this historic meeting, Emery and Trist discovered that putting the agenda in a larger context helped people transcend their conflicts. Emery had read the work of social psychologist Solomon Asch (1952) on the conditions under which people in groups will maintain their independence (Principle 6). From Asch's research, he derived criteria for productive collaboration. People need to experience that they (a) live on the same planet, subject to the same laws of nature, and (b) share the same psychological and physical needs.

When this happens, concluded Emery, "My facts and your facts become *our* facts." People can now dialogue about a world that includes all views, enabling new connections. Emery advocated a dialogic process that he called "puzzle-solving," putting the pieces of the elephant together to complete a rich picture of the aircraft engine industry that not one of the executives had before. Emery and Trist set out to design the course accordingly.

They would have the executives experience that all lived on the same planet and had the same needs. To accomplish this, they planned a day exploring global trends affecting everyone, followed by a day on the aircraft engine industry. They would then have participants face their shared needs for security and meaning in work. Only then would they move to make a strategic plan.

To enlarge the executives' horizons, they had outside experts join the group each evening for dinner, a speech, and a dialogue. The experts included an economist, philosopher, political scientist, army general, and theologian, each bringing a relevant bit of external environment or wise words on leadership.

Emery facilitated. Trist was the "process observer." As colleagues of group pioneer Wilfrid Bion at The Tavistock Institute, the pair assumed that groups faced with complex matters would react in predictable ways (Bion, 1961). They would avoid the task (flight), get into unproductive conflict (fight), or abdicate to the leader (dependency).

Trist's job was to stop the action if people abandoned the task. Much to his surprise, he had little to do. The executives were deeply engaged in dialogue on the state of the world and every aspect of the engine business. Trist and Emery had made a remarkable discovery. Exploring the whole before acting on any part, it seemed, helped the executives contain their anxiety about differences. Focusing on a task outside themselves, they cooperated to an unexpected degree, reducing the group's tendency toward fight, flight, and dependency.

Years later Fred Emery described in a letter to Marv how the meeting led to a small four-engine jet, the BA-146, that could get in and out of short fields at high altitudes. The company created its innovative power plant by building up a holistic view of aviation in a world of increasingly rapid change.

The Systems Revolution

In the years that followed, people applied systems think-ing to many organizational dilemmas. Applications often became complex intellectual exercises. These included such procedures as detailed maps of "environmental de-mands and constraints" in management training or strate-gic planning with high-level executives. The exercise required sophisticated thinking and the mastery of such abstract terms as *equifinality*, *negative entropy*, and *perme-able boundaries*. This was heady stuff for some but not readily accessible to people on factory floors or in commu-nity meetings.

There is a way, however, for you to benefit from sys-tems thinking in your meetings without ever employing the vocabulary. By following Principle 1 with Principle 3, you can make everybody systems "doers." Here's how. Conceive of your organization, community, network, or group as a system that exists in an "environment." A system's environ-ment is the place were it gets resources for survival—money, customers, clients, ideas, technology, and information. People must go outside themselves for sustenance if they want to keep their system alive. You can only change a system by changing its relationship to the outside world (Ackoff, 1974).

The same is true of meetings. If you use a meeting to bring "the environment" into the room in the form of peo-ple rather than squiggles on flipcharts, you open the door to action reverberating throughout the whole.

We are suggesting something more radical than talk—making systems thinking experiential rather than just con-ceptual. We are suggesting that if you have key people usually considered "outside" (e.g., part of the environ-ment), *and* you tap into what every person knows before acting, people will act systemically without being told that they should. People learn that together they can do things none would have considered alone.

—EXAMPLE—
Tremendous Trifle in the Computer Room

"I was working with people who run the computer room in a large insurance company," said consultant Billie Alban. "They took tapes on and off the machines and called themselves 'tape apes.' I wanted them to experience how important they were. If tapes were late, it affected every person's job." Billie got the computer workers together with vice presidents from the major departments. She had the group simulate what would happen if tapes were late. They discovered, among other things, the company could lose big contracts. If the system went down, said a VP, it could destroy their reputation and the business.

At that point, an hourly worker observed something that nobody had considered before. "On the console," he said, "there's a button that if anybody knocks it accidentally it could shut down the system over the entire country." At lunchtime workers went out, bought some plastic, and created a shield to protect the button. Only now, everybody from top to bottom knew they were protecting the whole company.

The Whole Elephant, Inside and Out

We are concerned not only with the elephant's environment and observations. We also care about its values and emotional life. In applying our techniques, we never seek to limit the way people express themselves. So when we say "whole elephant," we are thinking about what people see out there, what their world means to them, how they feel about it, and what they are doing now. We also are interested in what, if anything, they are willing to do.

If you choose to "explore the whole elephant" in your meetings, keep this key point in mind. It doesn't matter what techniques you use. Any method will work that fulfills the "Asch conditions," enabling everybody to talk about a world that includes all of their perceptions.

TECHNIQUES FOR EXPLORING THE WHOLE

From more than 20 years of experimenting, we have come to rely on four procedures that enable conversations on the nature of the whole. You can adapt them to many kinds of meetings. They are "go-arounds," time lines, mind maps, and flowcharts (process maps). These procedures serve multiple purposes. They get everybody talking about the same world; they enable every person to contribute (if they wish), making for a more level playing field; they make apparent the relationship all have to their task; and they encourage people to differentiate themselves, making integration more probable.

Many people attend a lifetime of meetings without ever experiencing these meeting dynamics. For that reason alone, activities like these represent a high order of change. Every person in the room learns more about the whole in a few minutes or a few hours than any one person knew coming in. There is no better way to invest your time.

1. Apply a "Go-Around"

The go-around can be used anywhere, any time, for quickly getting a lot of information from each to all. You simply have every person willing to speak say something in turn about a topic. We usually start meetings with a go-around, asking people for their names, affiliations, and why they have come. By using this procedure, we validate every person's views, check expectations, and give all a sense of where others stand. We begin building a community where every person's presence is acknowledged.

Don't minimize this practice. Consider the case of Carol Bartz, board chair of the international software company Autodesk, who attended a meeting of business and political leaders in Washington, D.C., where people did not introduce themselves. The men at her table assumed she was an office assistant. "Happens all the time," she commented (Cresswell, 2006). Well, it needn't happen in your meetings.

An initial go-around can also be used to set or amend an agenda. People can speak in sequence, or they can speak when they wish, continuing until everyone is heard. If you are using a cordless microphone, the mike serves as a "talking stick" when passed from hand to hand.

You can stop a meeting at any point where people bog down in ambiguity, conflict, or confusion, and ask to hear from every person, another way of saying to differentiate themselves.

The go-around is especially useful for

- reducing the fantasies people build up about strangers they have not met before;

- helping everyone know where others stand before making a decision or seeking to solve a problem;

- getting a stuck group moving when you are not sure what to do next;

- testing someone's assumption.

—EXAMPLE—
Does the Museum Have a Future?

The staff of a small museum showcasing a city's diverse cultures was concerned about the drop in attendance. They wondered how to raise this significant issue in a way that would draw on the board members' experience while giving everybody a new understanding of the museum's precarious situation. After 30 years of local development, many cultural events competed for attention. Board members were only dimly aware of significant changes affecting their institution. Each had their own connections—to banks, foundations, businesses, and social agencies—and knew that the city was on the move. Staff members experienced a daily erosion of their own influence.

At a regularly scheduled 2-hour board meeting, the president, on a consultant's advice, asked each board member to talk briefly about the changes taking place in his or her own organization and what implications this might have for the museum.

As each board member spoke, a portrait emerged of competing events and attractions. Within 30 minutes, the 25 people in the room all had a much richer picture of city activities than anyone had had at the start. More, they realized that a change in direction was essential to their survival.

The go-around can also be used on the spur of the moment any time people find themselves springing into action without fully understanding the situation.

—EXAMPLE—

"Everybody Here Is Unhappy . . ."

During a lunch break, a group of workshop participants held an impromptu meeting to complain to each other. The workshop leaders, happening to pass by, heard angry voices and heated comments that mentioned them. They asked if they could join in. One group member started by saying, "Everybody here is unhappy that you are not giving us concrete steps to follow. So far we only have general principles and nothing solid."

A workshop leader said, "We'd like to hear from each one of you before we respond. Is ____ speaking for all of you?" One by one group members gave their version of the story. About half the group was satisfied with how things were going. They had joined the meeting to find out what was going on. Of the rest, people had varying concerns, ranging from environmental (room too hot), to participation (not enough small group work or too much small group work), to eagerness to practice immediately instead of later as scheduled by the leaders. It turned out that only a few people shared the most vocal speaker's concern. "Well, then," asked the leaders, "what should we do?" The group decided to stick to the agenda with small modifications. The issue was resolved in a few minutes to everyone's satisfaction.

2. Use Time Lines

We use time lines to learn from the past, find patterns in the present, and discover implications for action. A time line consists of a strip of blank paper, vertical or horizontal, with key dates posted at intervals. We learned this method from the late Ronald Lippitt. In our version, we use long rolls of plain paper, 2 feet wide (0.61 meter), available in any stationery store. We cut strips from the roll (up to 24 feet or 7.32 meters) and put them on walls around a room. We label each strip with a topic (e.g., Health Care in X; Organization Y; Community Z) and add time frames at 5-year intervals. With small groups you can use shorter strips of paper.

Each person writes or draws pictures on the lines. Then small groups compose a story based on their reading of one of the lines. We always ask people to tell us what their story means for the work of the meeting. We can use one time line or several, depending on how many levels of a system we want to explore at once (e.g., individual, organization, sector, nation, the world).

—EXAMPLE—
Preserving Freshwater Fisheries

A fishing tackle trade group sponsored a 50-person conference of organizations concerned with sport fishing in freshwater lakes and streams. The participants—equipment makers, charter boat captains, anglers, writers—had never met together and were skeptical that they had anything in common. The group was puzzled when Dick Axelrod, the meeting manager, asked them to create two time lines, one a recent history of sport fishing and the second of the experiences that had led them into their work.

Within an hour, the group had achieved two valuable insights into the sport fishing world that none had ever got before. Though their problems varied by region, all were concerned that for fishing to remain a viable sport they had to protect the environment. They also found a common bond none could have predicted: Many had unconsciously chosen their careers years before in a similar way, finding that fishing was a satisfying time to be alone with their fathers. All were bound together by a wish to pass this legacy to future generations.

If you use this method, be aware that the more time lines you have, the more time you need. Don't overload people by piling on questions. The lines already contain rich, complex information. One or two questions will stir up all the conversation you can handle.

3. Make a Mind Map

The third technique we use for exploring the whole elephant is a group mind map, derived from the work of creativity expert Tony Buzan (1991). Mind mapping can be used for any purpose, from brainstorming to problem solving and decision making. It can be done in as little as 15 or 20 minutes, followed by as much conversation as you have time for. Larger groups may need 45 minutes.

We use a sheet of paper 6 feet high and 12 feet long (about 2 by 4 meters) if there is enough wall space. In the center of the sheet we put the meeting topic and circle it. Then we have people brainstorm trends in society that affect their topic now. We define a trend as a direction of change,

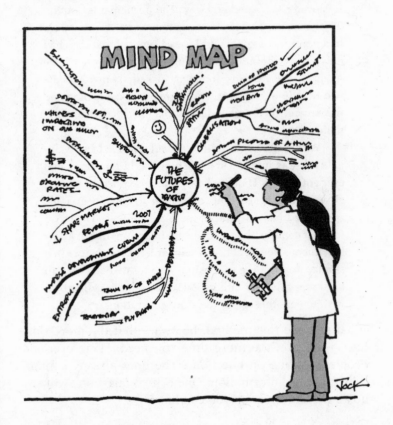

from more to less, from smaller to greater, and so forth. (You could as easily note causes, elements, characteristics, needs, stakeholders, symptoms—just about anything.)

Each new item is written on a new line coming off the circle or tied to an existing line. The person who names the trend indicates where it goes on the map.

All trends are valid—that is, legitimate to put on the map. We ask for concrete examples so that every person will know what the speaker is thinking. If somebody says, "Health care is getting worse," we ask for an example. "I had to wait 4 hours with my child in the emergency room last week." Somebody else may say, "I think health care is getting better. I had a heart bypass that saved my life." Both statements are legitimate, and both go on the map.

The purpose of this activity is to develop a view of the world that includes all perceptions. All conversations that follow will be in relation to the same world—the one that includes every trend on the map.

4. Draw a Group Flowchart

You can use a flowchart any time you are trying to understand a sequential process, such as making a product, organizing a fund-raising campaign, or delivering a service. This technique works best with systems where each step follows from a previous one. In a customer service department, for example, the sequence might start with a phone call. A service rep answers the call, asks for a name, a phone number, or other identifier, and pulls up the caller's record on a screen. The request is entered and then passed, if needed, to appropriate others. The call might precipitate any number of steps, from checking a shipment date, to issuing a return order for a product.

The flowchart would include contingencies for steps to take if (a) the caller is new to the system, or (b) key information is missing, or (c) a new shipment is required, or (d) an on-site service call must be arranged. The more possible steps in the sequence, and the more complex the system, the more possibilities there are for errors known only to one or two people but affecting everyone. Experts can and do create these charts of complex systems, in both designing them and troubleshooting them.

However, if your goal is to have the system understood by every person in it, so that each person can become a responsible troubleshooter, your best bet is to make a group flowchart. This means getting the whole system in the room to chart the system together. Each person describes a step, and each step is written on a large paper on the wall where everybody can see the whole. The key questions are "What happens first?" and "What happens next?" and "Then what happens?" If at any point nobody knows what comes next, we stop the exercise and ask, "Who knows?" Then we send for the person who knows. Nobody can understand the whole until the missing piece is put in place.

—EXAMPLE—
The Endless Paper Trail

A company making lifesaving cancer therapy machines had complaints from hospitals about long delays in getting replacement parts. Having no desktop computers (this happened long ago), the managers convened a small task force to speed up the process. The employees made a flowchart starting with the order taker on the telephone. As they traced their system, they discovered a fact that astonished everyone. Spare parts requests moved across 21 desks in 3 buildings before emerging, 2 weeks later, as shipping orders in the warehouse. Numerous forms were filled out, requisitions initialed, and approvals sought, an incremental accumulation of procedures over many years.

"How long does it take when a life is at stake?" asked a consultant. "In that case," said one employee, "we hand-carry it through the system and get it shipped the same day." The task force decided that the exception ought to be the rule. Working with all the people involved, they reduced the number of required steps from 21 to 5 and made 24-hour turnaround the standard for parts shipments. (Today such orders would be on their way within an hour of being placed.)

If you go this route, recognize that you cannot easily set a time limit for documenting a system unless you have all key people present. The more complex the system, the more time you need. Moreover, there are many wrinkles that can be built into or off this process. Often, the chart is used to trigger a "variance analysis," a detailed look at which errors crop up where, and how often. Such analyses may be essential for redesigning systems that no longer work. (For more details, see Weisbord, 2004, chapter 18, "Designing Work.")

DON'T CONFUSE TECHNIQUES WITH PRINCIPLES

Do not be misled by the techniques. The items on flipcharts read the same way no matter how they got there. The larger point is to use techniques that explore the whole elephant before coming to decisions. That way people make important shifts inside themselves before the words reach the flipchart. If you bring in the expert's process map without letting people modify it based on their experience, you defeat the purpose. If you jump too quickly to action planning, you may find people struggling to discern their positions, commitments, values, perceptions, and biases anyway, but with no systematic exploration. The chances for follow-through go way down if people talk past each other or continue to use different frames of reference.

Facts versus Opinions

"What is the role of facts versus opinions?" one of our reviewers asked after reading this discussion. This seems to
us an age-old debate that this book cannot resolve. Opinions are facts, not in the scientific sense but in the sense
that those who hold them act as if they are true. Moreover,
facts can be extremely flexible. We have seen "hard data"
used to prove any point anybody wishes to make. People
cite the research, news stories, and speeches that suit
them. That is what we have done in this book. We expect
you to do the same. In meetings people always are faced
with a philosophical choice. They can act on what they
have, keep talking, seek more data, or forget the whole
thing. We advocate mutual learning to the point where
people can make informed choices. That's the best anybody can do.

Principle 3: In Summary
....

Everything is connected to everything else. The best way
to find all the connections is to hear from people who have
firsthand experience. Find out what every person has
to contribute. In a short time, all participants will have
a more realistic and complex view than any one person
had at the start. Get everybody on the same page before
asking them to problem-solve or decide. They will make
better choices and be more likely to accept responsibility
for action.

Suggestions for Your Next Meeting

- Use a go-around to hear from every person on a matter of consequence.

- Based on your goal, try a time line, mind map, or flowchart. See whether you can get a picture of the whole that no one person had before.

- Try holding off problem solving and/or decisions until you are satisfied that all aspects have been explored.

Let People Be Responsible

*The owner of a shipping company ordered up a new oil tanker.
He employed the late Gunnar Hjelholt as consultant to lead
the ship's crew in designing a new work system. None had
ever shared decision-making, and they struggled through
several meetings. They wanted Gunnar to tell them what
they should do. "My comment," he recalled, "was, 'Who is
responsible for this ship?'"*

—Madsen & Willert, 2006, p. 252

There are many forces in society and in us that work against
people taking responsibility for themselves. We defer to
people in power; we look to experts for solutions and magi-
cians to entertain us; we sink into self-doubt when facing
ambiguity and seek heroes to insure our safety. No wonder
people expect anybody who leads a meeting to do most of
the work for them.

In this chapter, we present a philosophy for leading
meetings in a way that encourages participants to share
responsibility. Many people have proved its efficacy in diverse cultures. To get to this place, we have had to drop
cherished practices going back decades. We now get more
done in meetings, whatever their length, than when we believed that everything hinged on us. Whether you reject or
embrace our philosophy, we predict that you will be more
mindful of your own assumptions any time you lead others.

Paradoxically, to work the way we shall recommend means to stop worrying about what people will or won't do.

SHARING RESPONSIBILITY

Here are six ways to help people to share responsibility for a meeting and its outcomes. See whether they resonate with you.

1. Accept That Everybody Is Doing the Best They Can

If you can make this assumption your own, you will worry less and accomplish more. Suppose you truly believed that whatever people do in your meetings is the best they are capable of at that moment. What if you saw your impatience, perfectionism, judgments, and stereotypes as bottlenecks keeping people dependent? Suppose you decided that instead of pushing the river, you would clear the debris and watch it flow. What would you do differently?

Years ago we learned that we were ignorant of whole spectrums of human experience, much of which sat before us in meetings. Not only that, there was a lot about ourselves we didn't know. We were tempted to analyze other people's motives. Nothing reduces anxiety like putting a label on something that bothers you. We found the list of diagnoses daunting. Every book and workshop brought new categories. There were more ways to describe human behavior than stars in the galaxy and grains of sand on the beach.

- "They are in denial, because they don't want to be blamed for failure."

- "He'll do anything for attention."

- "She's afraid of looking bad."

- "He's passive"

- "She's aggressive."

- "They're out to sabotage the meeting."

- "They are victims of cultural myopia" (or sexism, or racism, or ageism, or whatever you fear).

When you act on these diagnoses, you move into risky territory. You may be right, wrong, partly right, partly wrong, or simply in Wonderland with Alice. The more diverse a group, the more interpretations there are for any bit of behavior, and the more likely you are to miss the mark. No map fits the whole territory.

Some years back we decided that if we were going to look for defensive behavior, we would find it everywhere. Then, we might never get down to work. Ditto resistance. Once you commit to leading people as you find them, you spare yourself a lot of anxiety and conserve your energy for doing what you are able to do. There is something about accepting others just the way they are that contributes greatly to community and builds trust. You can then make the purpose, goal, and task the driving forces.

People only do what they are ready, willing, and able to do. That is all you have to work with. A colleague of ours was facilitating an intense discussion among a global corporation's top executives. "People had so much energy," she reported, "they didn't even stop for a break." Suddenly everything came to a halt. Everyone stopped talking and averted their eyes. "The CEO looked at me to do something," she continued. "My thoughts began racing. *They're not being honest with each other. They've hit a wall and are backing off. I have to do a summary to help them get unstuck.* Instead, I asked, 'What are your thoughts at this point?' A voice from the back piped up, 'Hey, we need a bathroom break!'"

Learning from the Weirs

We owe our philosophy of action to the remarkable insights of John and Joyce Weir, friends and colleagues, who for more than 50 years ran personal growth workshops in "self-differentiation." We have applied the Weirs' philosophy in meetings around the globe, watching people do much more than we or they had reason to expect. The Weirs never urged anybody to do anything they did not want to do. They remained committed, engaged, enthusiastic, and available. They voiced no judgments on when, whether, or how people should involve themselves. Their only injunction was that you do nothing to injure yourself or another. Whatever other limits you came up against you put on yourself.

"Everybody," said the Weirs, in a phrase that informs all of our work, "is doing the best they can with what they have every minute of every day." Acting on that premise, we learned a great deal about our own and others' capabilities. In the end, we concluded, self-acceptance matters most of all.

2. Let People Hide Their Hidden Agendas

We content ourselves to let hidden agendas stay buried if that's where people want them. We do not ask people what they are *not* saying. We see this as a form of subtle coercion that undermines a group's willingness to accept responsibility. If people wish to conceal their "real" feelings or "real" data, that is a choice they must live with. Their choice is, for us, the real data. In our philosophy, people have a right to hold back.

The world keeps turning even if some things never surface. If we make it our job to remove every roadblock, we deprive people of responsibility for themselves. The world is full of people who have their own ways of getting by. So we encourage but don't demand openness. Our philosophy is that the driving force for a meeting ought to be its purpose. We hold ourselves responsible for keeping the task front and center. We push into sensitive areas only when we are invited to do so and believe that the issue is directly related to the achievement of the goal. The test for us is whether people keep working on the task despite what they hold back.

—EXAMPLE—
Who's Gorilla Is It, Anyway?

The founder–executive director of a successful nonprofit asked us for help in reorganizing. The agency had grown in 30 years from a local office to 2,000 employees in several states. While planning with us and his staff for a reorganization meeting, the director let drop that he was thinking of retirement. The staff seemed glad that he had brought it up; no one asked if he had a timetable or succession plan.

As the meeting date approached, we asked the director how he would handle his retirement plan in the upcoming meeting. He said he had nothing specific to offer but certainly would address the issue if it came up. The agency prided itself on its open climate. Before the meeting, we had heard hallway chatter about the director's plans. Did he have a successor? How would the transition be handled?

The meeting of 60 people from all levels went off without a hitch. The director involved himself fully, encouraging people to think and act "outside the box." During 2½ intense days, people decentralized their corporate offices, setting up teams to deal with far-flung programs. Nobody said the "R" word. Near the end, we wondered if we ought to get out in the open what was on everybody's mind. When we asked the director during a coffee break, he smiled enigmatically. We concluded that if no one saw fit to name the 800-pound gorilla in the room, then neither would we. It was not our gorilla. Five years later, the director was still talking about retiring, the organization was still growing, and people still buzzed in the halls.

Reluctance to Speak Does Not Always Mean "Hidden Agenda"
We make it a practice to invite individual comments after small groups report to each other in plenary sessions. In some cultures, people are energetic and vocal in small-group dialogues but are reluctant to speak out in large groups for fear of embarrassing themselves or being seen as pushy. In those cases, after everyone has heard small-group reports, we ask people to talk once again for a few minutes in their own small groups. We then ask for comments on what people have learned or noticed. Now the information is all made public while individual comments are cloaked in anonymity.

3. Do Less So That Others Will Do More

If you want others to take responsibility, we urge you to try doing less than you are used to doing. Nature hates a vacuum. When you step back, others come forward. If you believe everyone is doing their best now, you will not need to make them better. The biggest challenge we face as a species is learning to work with one another just the way we are—shortcomings, style defects, prejudices, and all.

Each time you move to fix a person or grou~~p~~
someone of the chance to do something const

The only way to find out how much people   ~~_~~ on
is to give them opportunities they never had. ᴛhe more
you busy yourself—explaining, rationalizing, interpreting,
justifying—the less room there is for other people. They
will sit back, watch you work, and evaluate your style.
Should you get into what's eating them, they may fight
back, requiring you to become a resistance expert. That is
a zero-sum game that takes people far from their task.

There was a time when we did all of the writing on
flipcharts, organized people's issues into categories, and
summarized what was said. Now, we invite group members to cluster, edit, and organize their own information.
There was a time when we put handouts on every chair.
Now we put them in a prominent place and invite people
to help themselves.

Restrain yourself from making decisions that affect
everyone, whether it's a change in the schedule, a task, or
the agenda. Preempting people's choices may have unintended consequences. Some people abdicate all decisions
and become more passive. Others fight the decision at the
expense of the goal.

—EXAMPLE—
"This Is a Waste of Time!"

Shem Cohen was helping a 40-person nonprofit group
plan a capital campaign. The meeting began with a review of the organization's history. Suddenly he found himself confronted by two angry participants. "They wanted
to skip most of the day's agenda and get right to action
plans," he recalled. They said their time was being wasted.
The emotionality seemed all out of proportion to the
situation.

"I told them that I appreciated them bringing their
concerns to me and that we needed to consult with the

whole group." Shem put the decision to everyone. After 15 minutes discussing pros and cons, all agreed to continue as planned. "The best outcome for me," he continued, "was that the people who brought up the issue felt heard and agreed to stay engaged. I was prepared to scrap the design if that's what most people wanted."

4. Encourage Self-Management

The advice that follows applies to those who take a facilitator role. If you are a manager reading this, you might consider the implications when you choose to lead a large-group meeting yourself or hire people to run such meetings for you. Assigning additional facilitators to each small group in a large-group meeting has an unintended consequence. It deprives groups of a chance to take responsibility for themselves. Most small groups can organize their work without formal leaders or facilitators.

A Helpful Mechanism One helpful mechanism that we offer when working with several small groups is a "self-manager guide." We suggest but do not insist that people take roles as recorder, reporter, timekeeper, or discussion leader. If you have groups of eight, half the people in the room are always in leadership roles. That's a big burden off of you!

What If Small Groups Have Trouble? We also know that some small groups don't click. We have made a philosophical choice to stay out when people are managing themselves. We don't go looking for problems. If a small group is struggling, we become involved if they invite us. Otherwise, we stick to managing conversations among the whole. We believe there is a learning curve in self-management. Our job is to be patient and provide support. This is not simply a meeting management issue. Inviting

small groups to be responsible can have larger consequences for a system.

—EXAMPLE—
Encouraging Employee-Owners to Take Charge

Netafim, owned by three community collectives (kibbutzim) in Israel, develops, sells, and implements irrigation systems. In the early 2000s, its management set out to get employees, most of whom also were owners, to accept more responsibility. Assisted by their consultants, Avner Haramati and Tova Auerbach, they organized an "open space" meeting in which group members propose and organize their own agendas. They invited "the whole system"—for example, employees, workers, board members, and managers from abroad. After one self-managed session on "enhancing innovations," an employee-owner started a department for innovations that increased the company's patent flow the next year. "People don't complain anymore," said one manager. "They either initiate and act or remain silent. They know that the road is open for them to take a lead on issues that bother them."

5. Contain Your "Hot Buttons"

One way to help yourself hold back is to pay attention to your internal critic, the little voice in your head that expects, insists, demands that meetings be perfect, that goals be clear, that each person behave with decorum, that anxiety dissolve into laughter, that enmity turn to support, that presentations be short and pointed, that questions be insightful, answers terse, action steps as inevitable as night following day, and, should any of these things *not* happen, it is *your* fault. Your internal critic, alas, wants what it cannot have. You will get more of what *you* want when you turn off the little voice. At the very least, turn down the volume.

Effective restraint requires us to work on ourselves. We have learned a great deal about leadership from studying our own inner impulses—to be perfect, look good, fix everything, be responsible for what people do or don't do. We urge you to do likewise. Your clues rarely emerge as a blinding flash of insight. Rather, notice those times when you get agitated, jiggle your knees, make faces, cringe at an untoward remark, or feel the impulse to contradict what you hear. Hold off a few seconds any time you want to jump in and correct somebody or challenge a statement.

—EXAMPLE—

Letting Provocation Be "Like Wind through a Tree"

A colleague was leading a strategic planning process for a successful professional group. At one meeting, he was confronted by a wealthy participant whose agenda was to control the organization. "The way he did it was through a personal attack on me," said our colleague, "since I had been contracted by the board to manage the process. 'Who are you?' he asked. 'What are you doing here? What kind of house do you live in?' All sorts of irrational things went through my head. *Yes, I wasn't as financially successful as these people (but they didn't know that). I didn't live in a mansion or routinely stay in five-star hotels!*

"Instead of defending myself and trying to convince people I deserved to be at the table, I let the remarks pass through me like wind through a tree. My first consulting principle is that the only thing I can control is my response to situations. I reiterated the goals of the meeting and asked if these were still relevant in light of the conversations to that point. I asked how they would like to proceed. When I ignored the bait, the person in question calmed down and participated productively for the rest of the meeting."

6. Encourage Dialogue

Make your meetings safe for dialogue. By *dialogue* we mean that those who wish to speak can say what they think, feel, want, or intend, while others listen. If discussion, debate, decisions, or solutions are called for, hold off until all those who want to talk have had their say. You will have a radically different experience in a meeting after all participants have expressed themselves on a topic than if you and others react to each speaker's views. You may never learn the range of perceptions in the room.

Dialogue Tops Intervention   People may not know their own stakes until they say them. People are more likely to change their behavior when they can hear others' perceptions and state their own without having to sell or defend them. At the start of each meeting, we tell people how important it is to hear from anyone who wants to speak. We emphasize that all ideas are valid. When we tell people it's OK to be wherever they are, we also are telling them that what they make of the meeting is up to them. Telling people that confusion, anxiety, and digression often precede clarity, excitement, and focus helps everyone feel less pressure. Seeking to establish that all ideas are valid, we provide a useful norm for defusing conflict.

—EXAMPLE—

Legitimizing Opposition in a Tense Community Meeting

"Last year I was working in a rural area," recalled meeting manager Lisa Beutler, "on an issue so contentious that the sponsor had security people to head off potential violence. I began the meeting with my ground rules. One, we are here because we want everyone's ideas, even things you may consider 'wrong' or 'silly.' You are not required to promote or defend your ideas. Two, everyone here has a right to change his or her mind.

"During the meeting, one person that security was keeping an eye on got up and said he needed to tell the group that 'Lisa, the facilitator, was trained in mind control techniques.' The group was flabbergasted and told him to sit down.

"Now I invoked the ground rules. 'This is what Jim is thinking right now, and you are not required to agree or disagree with him.'

"One woman said, 'I came a long way to this meeting to find some answers,' and others nodded agreement. People returned to the task. The disrupter (and his large contingent) got up and left. The community was still split over the issue, but this was a huge turning point. They didn't let the attack on the facilitator derail the meeting. Later I realized that by using the ground rule to cushion my own shock and to support the dissenter, the participants didn't have to get into a confrontation. They could put their energy into what they came for."

Principle 4: In Summary

You can encourage people to share responsibility for a meeting and its outcomes if you don't take the entire burden on yourself. One way to free yourself is to give up trying to diagnose individuals and groups, a task that grows more difficult the more diverse the group. Instead, learn to work with people the way they are. Make structure the focus of your attention rather than individual behavior.

Suggestions for Your Next Meeting

- Do less so that others do more. In the next meeting where something unexpected happens, just stand there. Pause. Notice your thoughts. Notice what your body wants to do. Then look around and make eye contact with as many people as you can. Find a person who wants to talk and nod in their direction.

- Accept that everyone does the best they can. Next time you hear a statement that bothers you, see if you can find a part of it with which you agree. Acknowledge it publicly or silently to yourself.

- Let go of hidden agendas. Instead of probing for what people are not saying, pay attention to what is being said. See what happens to your own assumptions.

- Use the self-manager guide. Try suggesting the four roles for self-managing an activity. If you are the leader, offer the timekeeper, recorder, and reporter roles to volunteers.

Find Common Ground

common ground, n.

- *"A foundation for mutual understanding"* (American Heritage Dictionary of the English Language, *fourth edition*)
- *"Shared beliefs or interests, a foundation for mutual understanding"* (American Heritage Dictionary of Idioms)
- *"A basis agreed to by all parties for reaching a mutual understanding"* (WordNet 2.0)

As you can see, dictionaries have reached common ground on *common ground*. They define it as the basis for mutual understanding. What they do not tell you is how to get there. That is the task of this chapter. We define common ground as those statements agreed to without reservation by every person in a meeting.

COMMON GROUND DIFFERS FROM COMPROMISE

Common ground is not compromise. When people agree reluctantly to propositions they consider partially OK, they end up endorsing positions they don't hold. Common ground does not require anyone to go along to preserve harmony. It describes real agreement at a point in time. Common ground also does not require convincing others that your views are correct. Talking long enough to "know what we are saying to each other" is the key to finding common ground. Nobody has to give up anything to discover that.

Common ground also includes acknowledging where you don't agree. When you identify "not agreed" items, you acknowledge every person's perceptions and validate unresolved issues. Disagreement becomes a reality to live with. People often use disagreements on item X as an excuse for not working together on items A, B, and C. Staying with where they *are* together helps people out of this conflict dilemma. They free themselves to cooperate on items of mutual concern. When some people agree and others don't, that is a reality to live with, not a problem to solve. All are still free to pursue their commitments, knowing the extent to which they have support. People are more likely to act quickly on items everyone wants. That is as close to reality as a group meeting ever gets.

BENEFITS OF FINDING COMMON GROUND

There are many benefits to finding common ground before solving problems or making decisions. Often you will save people a great deal of time, because

- ambiguity and uncertainty are reduced knowing where there is full agreement and where there isn't;
- energy can go toward implementation instead of convincing those who do not agree;
- people are more inclined to accept responsibility when they know where everybody stands;
- action is likely to be swifter;
- people are pleasantly surprised when they discover how much agreement exists.

GETTING TO COMMON GROUND

"Well," you say, "that all sounds very idealistic. But how on earth do you do it?" For one thing, you don't start a meeting by asking people what their common ground is. You might do that if they have been working together for months, but not if they are relative strangers. In most cases, you need to lay the groundwork by exploring the "whole elephant" to help people open up to one another (Principle 3). Here are further guidelines to make this exploration doable.

1. Hold Off Problem Solving

Save problem solving until all can talk about the same world. Everyone likes to have their problems heard, and one way to find out who shares them is to say them out loud. But rushing to solve problems too quickly diverts people from discovering what aspirations they hold. People may endorse solutions to move the meeting along and not follow through.

2. Get Conflicts into the Open, and Leave Them There

Seeking common ground reverses the 80/20 rule, for people often spend 80 percent of their time on 20 percent of the issues that they cannot resolve. When common ground is the goal, 80 percent of the time goes to finding where everybody is in agreement.

—EXAMPLE—

Transcending Conflict by Enlarging the Horizon

"I facilitated a series of meetings involving farmers, farmworkers, and housing developers in Washington State," recalled consultant Larry Dressler. "The governor charged a group with developing a master strategy for state-funded farmworker housing. The parties had a multidecade history of animosity and adversarial bargaining. A previous meeting ended with people accusing each other of 'intractable positions on which there would be no agreement.'

"When asked to facilitate the second meeting," Larry continued, "I formed triads consisting of a farmer, farmworker and developer. I asked them to interview each other using two questions: (1) 'Tell me about a time when you felt truly at home,' and (2) 'What does it mean to you to be involved in growing food eaten by people throughout the world?'

"Very quickly the participants discovered shared experiences and values linking housing and the work of growing food. Almost spontaneously, their discussion led to a set of 'must criteria for acceptable farmworker housing.' They found common ground through an 'appreciative inquiry' into two universal dimensions of human experience. This resulted in a strategy endorsed and actively supported by every member of the group."

3. Focus on the Future

Create an opportunity for people to tap into their deepest hopes and heartfelt dreams for the future. We believe that people aspire to bring meaning into every meeting. When given the space to translate their values into policies and procedures, they are often surprised how many others want the same things.

When a meeting calls for future scenarios, we ask people to put themselves X years in the future and imagine their dreams as if they have been realized; describe structures, policies, and relationships in the present tense; and look back on the single most important step they had to take X years earlier to get started. Dramatizing scenarios for each other, people nearly always come together on major goals. They also assimilate feelings of success to the point where they want to repeat them. In the book *Future Search* (Weisbord & Janoff, 2000), we describe these processes in detail. Many procedures, ours included, derive from the insights of the late Ronald Lippitt. He showed that looking backward from a "preferred future" while imagining what they *have* done motivates people more powerfully than asserting what they *will* do (L. Lippitt, 1998).

—EXAMPLE—
Backcasting from the Future

Ann Badillo, a business strategy consultant, uses a 2-hour "backcasting" exercise (in contrast to a forecast, where people stay in the present and look ahead). Each participant—as many as 40 at once—gets a large panel to backcast his or her future, imagining successes as if they have already occurred. "The room is filled with rich knowledge," she says. "By working *big*, everyone can see what others are doing. People work alone, then break into small groups to answer clarifying questions for about 45 minutes. Then the large group comes together to share patterns, themes, threads, and gaps. We dialogue in the round until the energy feels complete."

THE COMMON GROUND DIALOGUE

Once you have a desired future scenario, here are three options you can use to organize a common ground dialogue. Any one will suffice provided people have done enough work together to know where they stand. These activities can be done in short meetings or long.

Option 1. Start with Individuals or Small Groups

Have people work alone or in small groups to write down what they think every person in the room would agree to. Then have each person or group post its statements on the wall. Ask people to cluster similar items together. Then have volunteers read each cluster aloud. Ask for questions for clarification. If a person challenges the wording, ask the original writer what was meant. If all agree to small modifications, have a volunteer write a new statement. If, after a few minutes of dialogue, people cannot agree, move the item to a "not agreed" list.

Option 2. Work with the Whole Group at Once

Have people call out what they think everybody wants while volunteers write the items on flipcharts. (You can ask people to make notes alone first, if you wish.) Typical instruction: "Based on our conversations so far, what do you believe would be agreed to by every person in this room?" Then continue with reading and discussing each item in turn, as described earlier.

Option 3. Line Up Small-Group Easels (No Posting Required)

Have small groups each make a single flipchart of items they think all would agree to. Line the charts up in the front of the room. Have one person stand beside each chart. Ask the first person to read each item in turn from the chart he or she is monitoring. Ask the other monitors to cross off any duplicates they have. Do the same with each monitor in turn. When you get down to an unduplicated list, continue with a dialogue as noted before.

Turning Shorthand Lists into Complete Statements

The most important step is the dialogue after people's statements are posted. Dialogue is critical at this point because people use the same words to mean different things and different words for the same things. Nearly always, common ground lists are short items understood only by those present. As a final step, you can ask volunteers to write short statements for each item describing what this group intends. Sample instruction: "Write statements such that people who are not in this meeting will understand what you mean."

—EXAMPLE—

Washington State Department of Corrections

Grouped Items	Written Statement
Access to care	DOC provides offenders
Health education	with needed health care
Health care for offenders	services and access to treat-
Rehab services	ment and educational ser-
	vices that foster productive
	and law-abiding behavior.

Grouped Items	Written Statement
Document funding needs.	DOC expresses funding requests and decisions in terms of return on investment.
Manage to ROI	
Responsible money management	
ROI important	

Stay with Anxiety and Ambiguity

In our experience, the procedures described here will deliver 100 percent agreement on at least 80 percent of the items within an hour, even in groups of 60 to 80 people. Rarely will a group simply nod and agree. Nearly always, when people have a chance to dialogue, they discover nuances, shadings, and interpretations. Do not—we repeat—do not label this behavior "nit-picking." If you do, you underestimate what it takes for people to understand and commit to one another.

One reason there is so much cynicism about action plans rapidly agreed to and just as quickly shoved aside is that some people, to reduce anxiety, will go along despite misgivings. Avoid reinforcing this tendency when you lead meetings. Let people be anxious, and contain your own anxiety. (Principle 7 will show you how.) You'll end up with people knowing, often for the first time, where they truly are together and where they are not.

What to Do with "Not Agreed" Items Inevitably, there will be one or more items on the "not agreed" list. We always have these read aloud, too. We suggest you ask people if they understand the nature of their disagreements. Talk for a few minutes until they do. We are not looking for resolution, just clarity on the differences. If appropriate, ask people how they want to handle these items. At the very least document them. We are conscious that there are no perfect processes, and you can't tie up every loose end.

People can be responsible for their disagreements, too.

The test of the common ground method is the extent to which people are willing to follow through on items where everybody agrees. We always give people a chance to commit to the actions they will take and to due dates. We have noticed that sometimes it is easier to get agreement than action. Asked to vote on "what we *should* do" rather than "what we *will* do," people may list priorities they are reluctant to take on. In a community Future Search, for example, everyone readily agreed on the need to increase access to health care. Asked to vote with their feet—that is, to go and stand with others committed to do something about each common ground item—people chose other priorities. At action time nobody was ready, willing, and able to act on health care.

Finally, we iterate the obvious: lack of common ground does not exempt leaders with formal authority from making decisions. If you cannot get 100 percent agreement on an urgent agenda item, make the decision if you have the responsibility, or get a decision from the person who does. Be aware that you will have work to do to get others on board.

FROM CONFLICT TO COMMON GROUND IN ORGANIZATIONS

We come at last to organizational structures. An easy way to see a key dilemma of common ground in organizations is to revisit the classic D/I study of Lawrence and Lorsch (1967a) on how structural matters influence behavior. They compared more and less successful companies making similar products. They concluded that successful companies support necessary differences among departments and integrate their efforts despite inevitable conflicts. (Unintegrated differences lead to misunderstandings, competition, and conflict.) Their findings are especially relevant to internal staffers in quality, training, information technology, human resources, finance, and organization development. Staff work usually cuts across many departments. It is by nature integrative. People use expertise on behalf of the whole organization. Internal staff have much to gain from the proactive use of meetings.

Built-in structural dilemmas, however, work against integration. Every operating function carries with it different "task requirements" that people naturally observe if they wish to succeed. In a manufacturing firm, for instance, it is easy to see how Production, Sales and Marketing, and Research might come into conflict. Each has its own goals. Each works on a different time scale—short for Production, medium for Sales, and long for Research. And each has its own take on interpersonal skills—seen as critical by Sales and, in many cases, optional by Production and Research.

These are structural differences, related to the nature of the work. Structural conflict is the inevitable symptom of people holding onto orientations central to their identity. Unfortunately, departments can easily fall into the trap of attributing conflict to others' bad faith at worst, personal "style" differences at best. In such cases people's idiosyncrasies become the focus for action, rather than the problems that brought them into conflict. If you would find common ground, learn to recognize when conflict is also structural—that is, built into each department's tasks.

HOW TO GET CONFLICTING DEPARTMENTS ON COMMON GROUND

Here are three tips. Use these practices to help you take down "silos," reduce interdepartmental conflict, and bring diverse parties to common ground.

1. Depersonalize Conflict

Relatively few people realize the extent to which *structure* is a source of task conflict. People may stereotype, scapegoat, and exaggerate superficial differences to explain why they are right and others wrong. A self-fulfilling prophecy comes true as all parties do their best to bring out the worst in each another. To depersonalize conflict is to reassure the parties that they need their unique orientations to do their best.

Task conflict is more manageable than interpersonal hassles. Watch people relax when you tell them the strong feelings they have about their work are legitimate. *Of course* different goals lead to divergent expectations. *Of course* people with different deadlines march to different drummers. Note, too, how you relax when you decide to work with people the way they are rather than the way you wish they would be. (This is not an argument against interpersonal skills training. We need all we can get. Rather, we offer a structural context within which to view such training.)

2. Practice Effective Conflict Management

In their research, Lawrence and Lorsch found that when people smooth or avoid differences to reduce conflict, they undermine results. If they fight or force, they may exaggerate differences and reduce the effectiveness of the whole. Effective firms confronted issues and used problem solving for managing conflict, making differences and dialogue legitimate. "You believe this. I believe that." Only then could problem solving be effective. Be aware, though, that if conflicts have no easy resolution, keep the search for common ground front and center.

3. Be an Integrator Whenever Feasible

Lawrence and Lorsch (1967b) also discovered effective ways companies handled differences through the use of "integrators." These were product and project managers charged with gaining cooperation for an overall result. They found that good integrators could tolerate differences, making it a habit to acknowledge divergent needs without tipping toward either side of a conflict. Integrators who were seen as credible experts with no axe to grind could influence people for the good of the whole.

—EXAMPLE—
The Consumer Products Shoot-Out

The interdepartmental meeting in a consumer products company was in turmoil. Marketing had sent an angry memo that the factory turnaround times on Product X were unacceptable. The manufacturing manager had got together the relevant people to find out why. He was getting nowhere.

"We can't stand this lack of cooperation," said a marketer. "Nobody cares what it takes to make the product. Our job is keeping store shelves stocked."

"Well," said the manufacturing manager, "without us, you have no products to sell! It's not our fault that it takes us 8 hours to do a package changeover from Products Y or Z to X. Your customers want just-in-time deliveries. We can't move that fast."

As tempers heated up, we said, "Look, clearly it's in both your interests to keep production up and deliver on time. Let's all visit the packaging line and see what's going on." On the factory floor, a machine operator demonstrated why changeovers took so long. Product X required a different-size box from Products Y and Z. Every machine parameter had to be reset. "That's the box 'you people' insist on; that's the box we run!" said the operator to the salespeople.

Hearing this, the marketing manager was astonished. "We have no need for the boxes to be different," he said. He called the package designer, who said, "We thought sales required different sizes." He ordered an immediate redesign, production went up, and a major conflict went away. Three departments had found common ground at the packaging machine.

PUTTING IT ALL TOGETHER—SO FAR

The principles we advocate are not wholly independent. If you want to explore the whole elephant, you need "the whole system in the room." For people to find common ground, they need to be responsible for their own perceptions and agreements. You will find excellent examples of people taking responsibility for themselves in the Open Space meetings pioneered by Harrison Owen (1997). In these events, people are invited to organize their own conversations and to participate in as many sessions as they wish. Through a process of iteration and reporting to one another, groups come to discover their priorities. Many practitioners have found that the larger and more diverse the group, the more complete the picture everyone gets. Here's what can happen when you (a) get the whole system in the room, (b) control what you can, (c) explore the whole elephant, (d) let people be responsible, and (e) find common ground.

—EXAMPLE—

Diverse Citizens Agree on Community Priorities

Jean-Pierre Beaulieu led an Open Space meeting in a county of Quebec province in Canada with more than 100 citizens and several local mayors. To their surprise, they came to common ground on several priorities—for example, environmental protection, waste recycling, promotion of health through "good life habits," cultural tourism, and closer relationships between schools and regional employers (to reduce school dropouts). Such a result previously had been considered impossible.

"I think," said Jean-Pierre, "that people from different municipalities moved at the regional level when they realized that they shared so much unknown common ground. The meeting created a new dialogue among people that could not take place when each municipality was busy defending its turf. At the meeting's end, many people mentioned that this was the first time they had focused on life in the county as a whole. Several mayors said that the meeting would influence their future agendas and that they intended to be much more responsive to the voices of fellow citizens on the issues they had discussed."

Principle 5: In Summary

We define "common ground" as those statements every person will agree with after all views have been heard and disagreements made public. The major benefit of finding common ground is increased cooperation and fast action on matters of shared concern. When some people agree and others don't, treat that as a reality to live with, not a problem to be solved.

Suggestions for Your Next Meeting

- Pick an issue on which finding common ground matters. Tell people you want to treat problems and conflicts as information until everyone understands where they are together and where they are not. Create an opportunity for dialogue where people confirm their areas of agreement.

- Compile a list of those items that are "not agreed."

- Pick one of the three procedural options for finding common ground described on pp. 86–87, apply it, and see what happens.

Master the Art of Subgrouping

6

Why can't we all just get along?

> —RODNEY KING, commenting on riots that followed
> his beating by police on the night of March 3, 1991

Not long after World War II, a German refugee psychologist named Solomon Asch did a series of legendary group experiments. Asch imagined that an individual in a group faced with an obvious choice will choose correctly no matter what the others do. How wrong he was! He presented student volunteers with a line drawn on a card. They were asked to select an identical line from another card with three lines, two of them of different lengths. All but the "subject" were briefed in advance to give wrong answers. The subject disagreed repeatedly, becoming more agitated and uncertain. Within a dozen trials, most subjects went along with the group. Only one in four held out against group pressure although the correct line was obvious.

Years later we had the good fortune to visit with Asch and discuss his experiments. "I wanted to set up conditions under which every person could be independent of group pressure," he told us. He was surprised at how few held out against a group that clearly had it wrong. He thought the evidence of their senses would keep people steadfast.

UNTANGLING FROM GROUP PRESSURE

Seeking to free people from group pressure, Asch tried variations. He gave dissenters a (secret) ally briefed in advance to give an answer contrary to the majority. Now the subjects stood firm. The correctness of the ally's answers didn't matter. So long as one other person dissented from the majority, subjects stayed true to what they believed to be right. Asch then had the ally leave the room on a pretext. Most subjects reverted to giving answers they knew to be wrong. To maintain their reality, people needed support from another dissenter (Asch, 1952; Faucheux, 1984).

In this book, we identify what Asch did in his experiments as "subgrouping." He created two-person subgroups united by their dissent. Without support, few people could stay independent. Asch told us that he never imagined his findings would be applied to business meetings. In fact, he has opened doors to more effective meetings all over the world.

VALIDATING THE POWER OF SUBGROUPS

Now fast-forward two decades. Yvonne Agazarian (1997), developer of Systems-Centered group theory, was experimenting with the theory that groups develop new capacity as they discover and integrate differences. She found that when people make controversial statements, they risk being ignored, coerced, or attacked. Should that happen, people abandon the task, moving instead to their feelings about right and wrong. The way to keep groups whole and working on their task is to make sure that nobody becomes a scapegoat for saying something out of the ordinary.

In pursuing this, Agazarian gained new insights into the workings of dynamic systems. She found, for example, that she could organize informal subgroups for differences as they arise. People had the potential to manage conflicts effectively when they could identify with subgroups based on similarities. When there was a subgroup for every difference, so long as the groups didn't fight, people were better able to stay with a task. Moreover, when people discovered similarities among different subgroups, they became capable of integrated solutions to complex problems.

HEADING OFF GROUP SPLITS

We have adapted Agazarian's insights to task-focused meetings, using techniques we will describe. Heading off potential splits requires new behavior if you are not used to staying with tension when differences arise.

As you apply the theory outlined here to meetings, you will discover a wholly new way of keeping groups on task regardless of their differences. As you learn to do this, you will free yourself from needing to fix every problem that comes up.

You will not need to diagnose a group's behavior, its stages of development, or its members' personalities, nor will you need to confront any individual's behavior. You will become active only in those instances when disagreements might end productive work. Instead of dreading conflict, you may come to experience differences as a creative opportunity to keep people working without their having to agree.

A THEORY OF DIFFERENCE: WHY WE CAN'T ALL GET ALONG

What makes leading meetings a challenge is that nobody is indifferent to differences. We may hate them, love them, avoid them, or rub everybody's noses in them, but the one thing we are not likely to do is remain neutral about them. When a group starts poking at contrary views, dialogue may turn into dismissal or attack. The task goes out the window. Some may feel the need to convince others they are wrong; some may worry about hurting other people's feelings; some may start labeling others as "change resisters" or "touchy-feelies" or whatever comes into their heads.

Whether any of this is said or not, once these (largely unconscious) processes get under way, you can say good-bye to task focus, creative solutions, and committed implementation. When a topic is hot, what ought to be ordinary matters of fact—"You believe this; I believe that"—quickly become "my good views" versus "your bad ones." Those who feel superior start throwing their weight around, while those who feel inferior give up or rebel.

Frustration rises. How will you keep the lid on? When views collide, you may be tempted to smooth over the differences. We want to fortify you to respond to tension by moving toward it. Getting people to differentiate themselves—to heighten their awareness of their differences—holds the key to integrated problem solving and decision making.

WE UPSET OURSELVES OVER DIFFERENCES

One near-universal experience makes the practice we advocate a personal challenge for every reader of this book. From the days when our ancestors lived in caves, people have stereotyped without a moment's reflection other families, tribes, or villages. It is our lot to categorize people before we know them.

We walk into a meeting with strangers and gravitate toward people similar to us and away from those who are not. We judge people based on very little contact. This process is as natural as breathing. Much of the time our judgments do no harm. If we need to work with others, however, we may escalate first impressions into divisive stereotypes. Think how easily we dichotomize men and women, rich and poor, old and young, fat and thin, light skinned and dark, physically able and disabled, short and tall, sick and healthy, housed and homeless, working and unemployed.

The list never ends. And our negative predictions about "them" can turn deadly, as anyone can tell you who has lived in Northern Ireland, the Middle East, and parts of Africa. There, stereotyping begins with "Catholics are . . . , Protestants are . . . , Israelis are . . . , Palestinians are . . . , blacks are . . . , whites are . . . , Latinos are . . . , Asians are . . . , rich are . . . , and poor are . . ." and ends with vile attributions, hostility, and aggression persisting over centuries. To experience the tip of this iceberg, you need not go to places of hair-trigger conflict. Indeed, if you look hard enough, you may find some inside yourself. You also may encounter incipient aggression in any meeting.

—EXAMPLE—
"We Have a Thousand Jobs . . ."

We were managing a welfare-to-work meeting in a midwestern county to involve citizens in carrying out a new federal law. The meeting included bankers, business owners, social workers, county officials, and welfare recipients. People started with considerable goodwill as the sponsors spoke about the importance of finding solutions that would benefit families and employers, solutions that would take into account needs for training, transportation, and child care if full-time parents on welfare were to be employed.

Early on the welfare group told how hard it was for them to find work. Soon after, the employers announced that together they had 1,000 unfilled jobs.

"If you were really motivated," said one business owner to the welfare group, going on the attack, "you could easily get one of those jobs!"

A welfare mother rose to the occasion. "You have no idea what my life is like!" she shot back, anger building with every word. "I've applied for some of those jobs, and all your interviewer sees is my black face!"

In 15 seconds, building on stereotypes of each other, people were ready to fight. Our task was to help the stereotypical subgroups become functional. This we did by means that we will describe in this chapter. For purposes of this example, we can say that the turning point came after a long dialogue when another employer faced the angry woman and said, "You're right. I have no idea what your life is like, and I would like to know more."

Here we provide a way of understanding subgroup dynamics that will help you manage situations like the one just described.

SUBGROUPING GOES ON
ALL THE TIME IN MEETINGS

Every meeting provides a forum for mutual stereotyping, drawing on the best and worst parts of our psyches. (In Principle 8 we explore "projection" and how to free yourself from overdoing it.) No matter what formal structures you use, group members from the first moment will be drawn into invisible subgroups. Because people keep most projections secret, even those meetings that seem smooth and orderly become a jumble of unspoken wishes, energies, and frustrated impulses. Somebody forms a judgment and becomes part of a subgroup that includes every other person with similar thoughts. Of course, no one knows it unless you take the trouble to poll the group. There is at work an informal system functioning apart from the people in it.

On the surface, you have people doing what they do in meetings. Underneath, each person is aligning with, distancing from, or ignoring every statement made. Each audible remark becomes a focal point for new, invisible subgroups forming and re-forming from moment to moment. If a meeting were a cartoon panel, you would see little cloudlike balloons over each person's head. Inside would be unspoken comments like "That's the dumbest thing I ever heard" or "I'd never say anything like that!" or "This is a huge distraction" or "I'm glad he had the guts to speak up."

Rarely do people voice these thoughts. Most of us discover early in life the psychic risks of going against the group. When somebody heeds the impulse to do that, tension rises. Some manage their discomfort by hoping, even expecting, that the leader will take care of it. Others ask challenging questions. Others patiently explain how the deviant missed the point. Some practice a firm, friendly coercion toward their own view. No wonder so many people sit on ideas or feelings that might violate a group's unspoken norms.

YOU CAN TURN STEREOTYPICAL INTO FUNCTIONAL SUBGROUPS

Fortunately, just knowing this phenomenon gives you leadership options you never had. With a few well-chosen words, you can change a stereotypical subgroup into its functional equivalent. We use the adjective *functional* here to suggest "contributing to growth," not to describe people's jobs. Functional subgroups transcend the stereotypical subgroups that people form and re-form in their heads. The practice, derived from Yvonne Agazarian's work, is simple, fast, and effective.

Asch showed that so long as each person has an ally, people maintain their independence. Agazarian went further, demonstrating that so long as there is a subgroup for every viewpoint, every voice is heard, and people add new information, the whole group is more likely to keep working on its task. This point is so easy to miss that it bears repeating. So long as every person has a functional ally— somebody who carries the same ideas and/or feelings—a group is more likely to keep working. Members will not distract themselves with side trips into rejecting, rescuing, or scapegoating those who take risks. Our minimal job becomes helping people experience functional differences when stereotypes might prevail. If we do this job right, group members will take care of the rest.

Don't Just Do Something

When we lead meetings, we just stand there so long as people stay with the task by

- putting out their own ideas;

- asking questions;

- answering questions;

- asking for or giving information;

- building on each others' ideas.

We even stand there when people flounder, stumble, express confusion, wander off the subject, or dream out loud. Usually a group recovers quickly from occasional side trips. We believe that every contribution has value, even though it may not be obvious. Groups usually ignore a person's stumbling, and so do we. If the flow of conversation veers away for several comments in a row, we consider it our job to point that out. Typical comment: "Let's pause and see where we are. I think I'm losing the thread."

Now and then one of us will ask someone who seems to have wandered far alone and is at risk of not coming back, "I know there is a connection between what you are saying and the topic we're discussing. How does it connect up for you?"

Even when we seem relatively quiet on the outside, just standing there for us involves actively observing potential subgroups and their impact on the work.

FOUR KEY TECHNIQUES FOR FUNCTIONAL SUBGROUPING

When people say or do something that visibly heightens the tension, when we hear the crackle of fragmentation and splitting, fight or flight, we go on high alert. Those are the moments when we must be ready to act. Here we describe four key techniques that make up the core of our meeting management.

Technique 1: Ask an "Anyone Else" Question

This practice is stunningly simple. Act when you hear people make statements so emotionally charged that they put themselves at risk of being isolated or labeled. For example:

> PARTICIPANT: We have been at this for 2 hours, and I'm frustrated that we haven't made more progress!

We judge the impact of such statements by the extent to which tension rises in the group. Sometimes people jump in to challenge the statement, putting the speaker on the defensive. The temptation is to let the antagonists have it out while everybody watches. This can make an entertaining reality TV show. It rarely expedites the task.

You can do better. What is needed now is neither confrontation nor a search for "truth." Rather, you need to head off the split so that people keep working. The best way to do that is to get an informal subgroup for the risk taker. For many people, this will be counterintuitive. Rather than look for somebody who is not frustrated to counterbalance the first person, your best move is to get the frustrated person joined.

> LEADER: Anyone else feeling frustrated?

We expect one or more people to raise their hands. When they do, we ask for their experience. Usually we discover they have a spectrum of frustrations. Speakers see that they are not alone. Frustration is OK. Confrontation is avoided. Everyone has new information on where others stand. The group moves on.

Sometimes, however, people ignore the frustrated person, moving on to other topics, leaving emotionality hanging like fog in the air.

> LEADER (recognizing the unfinished feelings): I want to go back to what _____ said a minute ago. Is anyone else feeling frustrated?

We stop. We look around. We repeat the question if necessary. We watch for heads to nod.

LEADER (to those nodding): What do you experience?

One person gives his or her version. Perhaps another chimes in. At this point the group is working again. What might have been a fight becomes a dialogue on a key issue—the degree to which the work frustrates people. This is not a denial of the reality of the person who brought up the issue.

In the welfare-to-work meeting cited earlier, we allowed the confrontation between the employer and welfare mother to continue for a bit as tensions rose in the room. Before things turned really ugly, we moved to get the contentious parties into the same functional subgroup by asking, "Anyone else feeling deeply about this issue?" Hands went up around the room from all stakeholder groups. Now several people chimed in with their concerns, enlarging the subgroup. This paved the way for the employer who then asked to know more about the lives of welfare mothers.

By finding an ally, in effect creating a subgroup, we kept both the employer and the welfare mother from becoming scapegoats. We acted to help the group accept frustration rather than turn it into further aggression.

Rules for Asking "Anyone Else?"

1. Listen for the intensity of feeling, and note what happens in the group. Many statements require no response. The person making them is satisfied to get it out, and people accept the comment as part of the dialogue.

2. Cite the *content* of a statement only when the content does not threaten a personal attack or a divisive argument.

PARTICIPANT: I'm confused about what's going on right now.

LEADER: Anyone else confused? (Rather than "Let me explain it to you.")

3. Cite only the *feeling* behind the statement if the issue is potentially divisive. In other words, find a subgroup for the emotion, so that all emotions remain legitimate.

PARTICIPANT: I'm getting impatient with the idea that business is more important than anything else.

LEADER: Is anybody else impatient right now—for any reason?

Informal Subgroups Emerge during Meetings   Note that we can't anticipate functional subgroups. We discover them as the meeting progresses. It takes only one ally to form a subgroup, validate a person's right to an opinion, and keep the meeting on track. As people learn that there is a subgroup for every issue that matters, they are more likely to join the conversation and create a more realistic portrait of the whole. The "anyone else" question also preempts a habit that we often run into, somebody saying, "I'm sure I'm the only one who feels this way, but . . ." or "I know I speak for many others when I say. . . ." Whenever we hear this, we ask the person to ask if anyone else feels the same way.

In managing meetings, we need to emphasize, we are not standing there saying "anyone else" every few minutes. Even in meetings lasting 2 or 3 days, we rarely ask this question more than once or twice. We attribute this to the fact that we seek from the start to validate every person's experience. In our strategic planning meetings, for example, the time lines described in Principle 3 serve this function. When the context includes everyone, most groups then handle what comes up without fleeing or fighting. When groups come to recognize the power of joining, individuals will ask as a matter of course if anyone else feels the way they do. Indeed, if you are participating in a group, not leading, and wonder whether you are alone with a particular view, you can easily ask, "Anyone else?" rather than wonder. That is the best form of reality check. You keep yourself engaged by surfacing your own subgroup.

Suppose Nobody Joins?   In our learning workshops, somebody inevitably asks, "Suppose nobody joins?" Well, we have been there, too. Once in a great while—maybe every year or two—one of us will ask an "anyone else" question and be greeted by silence.

> PARTICIPANT: This has been a big waste of time for me.
> LEADER: Anyone else feel they are wasting their time?

Nobody says a word.

In that case, we see whether we can authentically join the person who has gone out on a limb. We may wait as long as 20 seconds after asking, "Anyone else?" which seems like an eon longer than eternity. When nobody speaks, tension builds while we consult our experience for an honest response.

LEADER: I've had moments here when I thought I was wasting my time, too.

Suppose we can't authentically join. The meeting has been great from our point of view.

LEADER: It seems you're the only one at this moment. Are you able to move on?

Technique 2: Use Subgroup Dialogue to Interrupt Polarization

Asking "Anyone else?" is not always the end of the story. Now and then people become deeply polarized over conflicting beliefs, problem definitions, solutions, or decisions. In such cases, people may strongly disagree without stereotyping each other, but their conflict threatens to derail the task. There is a second technique we use for instances that paralyze a group. Our objective is to have people explore both sides of the conflict, but not in the way you might imagine.

Instead of encouraging a dialogue between polarized subgroups, we stop the action and have people in Subgroup A identify themselves. We do the same with Subgroup B. Then, we encourage the A's to talk *with each other* while the B's listen. After all the A's have had their say, we ask Subgroup B to do the same while Subgroup A listens.

The reason for this may not seem obvious. When people dialogue with those who are ostensibly similar, comparing notes on what they believe and why, they nearly always discover differences that were not apparent at first. There is a spectrum of views within Subgroup A (just as members of a political party vote the same way for different reasons). Often this comes as a surprise to both Subgroups A and B. Moreover, when people listen in on conversations among those they consider different, they nearly always discover positions similar to theirs that they could not discern until now.

In short, we affirm Yvonne Agazarian's principle that within apparent similarities, differences always exist, and within apparent differences, similarities will emerge. As people make these finer distinctions, they develop a more grounded sense of what they consider relevant. They experience a continuum of opinions rather than two opposite poles. They suspend for the time being their stereotypes and projections and get on with the business at hand. Differentiation leads to integration. Both/and replaces either/or as the unspoken group assumption.

—EXAMPLE—
Mending a Split over Decision Making

In a business meeting, people split over what they believed were the principles underlying effective company decisions. Fact-based decision making ranked high for one vociferous participant. A VP hesitantly noted that feelings and intuition often entered into his decisions. The first speaker, surprised by this, heatedly asserted the centrality of facts. We asked her to find out if anyone else shared her view. Several raised their hands. Next, we asked who believed intuition and feelings entered in. Several other hands went up.

Two functional subgroups became visible. We asked each subgroup to explore thoughts and feelings among themselves while the other subgroup listened. Members of both soon found differences in their apparent similarities. One woman, for example, admitted that to stay fact based, she had to struggle to keep feelings and intuition out. On the other side, one man said, "Of course I pay attention to data, and I also use information that is not based on hard numbers."

The subgroups integrated their views by validating each other's stand under certain conditions. People later said they were astonished that no confrontation was necessary. Indeed, they had created a larger third subgroup,

SIMILARITIES — DIFFERENCES

those who could accept that this might be a "both/and" proposition. The whole exchange took less than 10 minutes.

Technique 3: Listen for the Integrating Statement

How do you know when a group is ready to take a next step? One clue is when people start recycling earlier statements. This usually indicates that a spectrum of views is now on the table. No one has more to add. An even more reliable sign that a group has all it needs to move on is what we call an "integrating statement." Polarized groups often get stuck in tense "either/or" conversations. An integrating statement takes the form of a "both/and" comment, recognizing that each side of a polarity has validity. When we wait long enough for a dialogue to run its course, a group member will nearly always volunteer such a statement.

—EXAMPLE—
An Age-Old Conflict—Environment or Jobs?

For most of 2 days, citizens of an economically troubled Washington State county had shared ideas for improving their future. As they got down to areas of agreement, a real estate developer rose. "You people," he said, addressing a watershed preservationist, "stand in the way of every project we try to get off the ground. As long as you stop progress, we will have no decent jobs."

Bob Woodruff and Bonnie Olson, the facilitators, felt the tension rise in them and in the group. "Several participants looked at us, as if to say, 'Aren't you going to do something?'" Bonnie recalled. The pair had disciplined themselves to "just stand there." The room fell into an awkward silence. After several seconds, another developer got up and pointed to an aspiration on the wall that all had agreed they wanted: "Healthy development that protects our natural resources."

"We all rely on our beautiful environment," he said, "*and* we all want good jobs in the area."

There was no need to ask an "anyone else" question. The energy in the room shifted as several people raised their hands to expand on or affirm the both/and statement. A tense moment passed. "Here was the integrating statement that dissolved the conflict," said Bonnie, "and it came from another developer. Bob and I breathed a silent sigh of relief."

Fortunately, we find many natural integrators in groups. Suppose no one comes forward? Well, in a pinch, we can always state the obvious. "We hear two points of view, A and B. What would you like to do with these?" When all else fails, we consult group members on what they want to do.

Technique 4: Get Everybody to Differentiate Their Positions

Throughout, no matter what else goes on in a meeting, we stay mindful that people can integrate only to the extent that they make functional differences public. People need to know who they're dealing with and what they bring to the table. If they don't, their apparent agreements could be perfunctory, superficial, and unlikely to stand up. We never run an interactive meeting without giving everyone a chance to comment on what they do, why they came, what they want, and/or what they know. In groups of up to 50 or 60, we nearly always start with a go-around. We might ask people for their name, role, and interest, for their expectations, or for their understanding of the goal. In larger groups, we might have several small groups do this simultaneously.

This technique also becomes a dependable security blanket when there is uncertainty about what to do next. We use the go-around any time we feel stuck and need to break an apparent logjam. We simply stop the action and say, "We'd like to hear one sentence from every person who wants to speak. How do you feel (or think) about situation _____? Then we will decide what to do." Nearly always this act of differentiation produces information that gives all of us choices not obvious a few minutes earlier.

Principle 6: In Summary
....

Functional subgrouping is the practice of inviting people to ally with others based on similar experiences, feelings, or points of view. Groups will keep working so long as no member becomes a victim of stereotyping. The way to head off fight or flight is to help people experience their differences as functional rather than stereotypical. We do this by invoking subgroups if scapegoating or splitting seems probable. In conflict situations, you can go further and form temporary subgroups in which people explore their positions. Most of the time they will resolve and move on when they discover a legitimate spectrum of views, making confrontation unnecessary.

Suggestions for Your Next Meeting

- Pay attention to a statement that makes you wish a person had stayed quiet or used different language. Decide whether to find that person an ally for the content or the feelings (see pp. 107–108).

- If you lead a group that becomes deeply polarized, stop the action and use a subgroup dialogue (p. 110). See if that frees them enough to move on.

- Try a go-around to start an important meeting. Ask people to say something that adds to everyone's understanding of the work they have come to do.

- Use a go-around to get clarity during a meeting where people are not sure what to do next. Note if the next step becomes apparent.

PART TWO

MANAGING YOURSELF

Make Friends with Anxiety

Get Used to Projections

Be a Dependable Authority

Learn to Say No If You Want Yes to Mean Something

These chapters speak directly to our core belief. While we cannot change other people, we have an obligation—if we aspire to lead others—to work on ourselves. So we offer some practices that we have adopted on the never-ending road toward becoming better leaders:

- Accepting anxiety as a natural and inevitable traveling companion when stakes are high, issues complicated, perceptions diverse, and answers uncertain (Principle 7)

- Becoming aware of the way projections (thoughts and feelings in us that we experience as located "out there") influence our behavior and the way that others react to us (Principle 8)

- Accepting that as leaders we inevitably draw "good" or "bad" projections from others and can increase our competence by working with this reality (Principle 9)

- Learning to say no anytime we believe we are in an untenable situation (Principle 10)

Of all these proposals, some early readers found our suggestions for getting used to projections (Principle 8) puzzling, unfamiliar, difficult, and perhaps unnecessary. Their reactions reinforce our conviction that we are on the right track in offering this material here. You will not find it in many places, and you can skip it if you feel overwhelmed. One definition of *change* is doing something you never did before. If you seek to improve your leadership skills, here is a chance—without anybody checking up on you—to discover some aspects of yourself enabling you to enhance your own development.

Make Friends with Anxiety

Nothing in the affairs of men is worthy of great anxiety.

—PLATO

Anxiety. Everybody has it. Nobody loves it. Mel Brooks made a movie about it, *High Anxiety* (1977). W. H. Auden wrote a long poem, "The Age of Anxiety" (1947), set in a New York bar. Leonard Bernstein adopted Auden's title for his Symphony No. 2 (1948). We are wallowing in anxiety, generalized, unfocused, nonspecific, and—our favorite term—*free-floating*, a kind of nervous cloud on which we depart the present in a sour mood for a place we'd rather not be. When we put the word *anxiety* into Google, we got 112 million hits in 0.07 second. That's a lot of free-floating anxiety in cyberspace.

ANXIETY—GETTING READY TO LEARN

This chapter has twin themes to help you manage anxiety when you lead meetings that matter. Our first theme is that task-related anxiety can be your best friend. The poet T. S. Eliot called anxiety "the handmaiden of creativity" (or so it says on the Internet). You, too, may discover that apprehension in a meeting often serves as a precursor to creative breakthroughs.

Our second theme is that anxiety provides a wonderful window into your own development. We have learned a great deal about managing our fears and fantasies while leading high-stakes meetings. You can grow your capability for leadership manyfold by increasing your tolerance for disorder, ambiguity, and tension. Often you do not need to know why you are anxious, only that you are. When a meeting falls into confusion, the urge to retreat or fix it immediately can be irresistible. Don't panic. You will help yourself immeasurably by hanging in despite your queasy feelings. If you wait just a while longer, you can help people find greater clarity and move in new directions.

WHAT DO YOU DO?

If you run meetings, you get a lot of anxiety, yours and others'. Somebody does something so outrageous that tension rises to the breaking point. You feel a chill creep up your spine, invade your belly, and clutch your throat. The room grows as quiet as Death Valley. Everyone waits for you to fix it. Whatever action you take, there is always a group expert waiting to tell you what you should have done. The loudest person will soon insist that this is not what "people" came for. Those most anxious of all, hoping caffeine will fix everything, want a break.

Surely, you think, there is something you could say that would make it all OK. Groups expect you to be an inspiring leader, a take-charge manager, and a supportive facilitator. They project fantasies on you—of parents, teachers, bosses, cops, and con artists. If you lead the meeting, you must know what to do.

How much of this do you expect of yourself? And how much of what you expect is based on what they expect? How can you learn to accept whatever you feel and carry on with constructive intent? How do you learn to reduce your own anxiety in tense situations? This chapter will help you answer these questions. If you can't avoid the anxious part of yourself, why not make your feelings work for you? As you succeed, you will find the capability for managing yourself in such a way that the groups you lead will do more while you do less. You will relieve yourself of a long list of shoulds, oughts, and have-to-do's that sap your energy, bog you down, stress you out, and hold others back.

Here are the perspectives on managing anxiety that we have found most useful.

1. Visit the "Four Rooms of Change"

Perhaps the simplest way to understand our point of view about anxiety is to spend a few minutes in our favorite virtual dwelling place, Claes Janssen's (2005) "four rooms of change." Janssen, a Swedish social psychologist, made an inspired leap in the 1970s. He devised a model of human development you can learn quickly if you are willing to reflect on your own experience.

For decades we have presented the following diagram at the start of interactive meetings. We have found it a great anxiety reducer for people to know that we do not know how to avoid anxiety and in any case consider it an

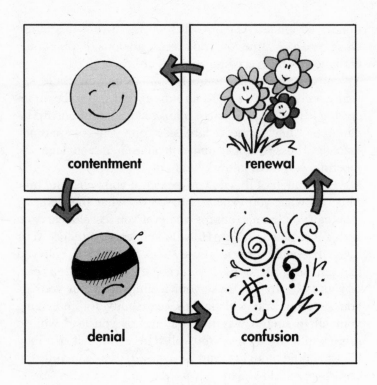

important milestone on the road to purposeful action. Moreover, Janssen's model helps us manage our own anxiety. As we have worked with it over the years, we have come to appreciate all of the rooms.

First, let us describe the rooms as we experience them. Then we will tell you how we introduce this model in meetings. Start in the Contentment Room, where everything is fine, the world secure, soft lights, music, and easy chairs. Why would we change anything? Pause. . . . Breathe deeply. . . . Relax. . . .

But then something happens! A thunderstorm. An earthquake. We interrupt this music to bring you a breaking story: fires and floods coming your way. We are inundated with messages we would rather not hear, over-whelmed with information we cannot absorb. We seek refuge. And the nearest way out is through the door marked Denial.

In the Denial Room, we hunker down on a hard bench in the corner. The room is windowless, the air heavy and hard to breathe. We sit on our feelings. We smile with tight lips. Deep down we sense that all is not right. It's better not to know. So we act as if nothing is happening. After a time, we may connect with some buried part of ourselves. We do not like this place. We are angry for having got into it. In fact, we're overwhelmed with feelings—fear, appre-hension, excitement, and above all the urge to move.

Suddenly we look around and realize that in our agita-tion we have fled Denial and gone through the door marked Confusion. Anxiety is the décor of the Confusion Room. Bright lights flash the colors of the spectrum. Music, sometimes louder than we can stand or softer than we can hear, stops and starts at random. We see walls cov-ered with writing we can't decipher.

We search for a way out. No exit strategy seems obvi-ous. There are several doors. Access to any one of them re-quires that we make sense out of chaotic images that boggle our brains, agitate our bodies, and deplete our spir-its. Unlike the Denial Room, though, now we have a lot to work with. We are aware that we want out. We know that we feel frustrated. As we struggle for clarity, new patterns emerge, possibilities we never considered until now.

Little by little, without our pushing on them, doors to the Renewal Room start popping open. Then, in a few mo-ments more, everything becomes possible. We choose a door and emerge into bright sunshine, fresh air, and a stimulating breeze. Roads beckon, lined with things to do and see that we never thought could be ours.

In the Renewal Room, everything seems possible. But wait! Is it? We must choose. Will we pick the city or the woods? The mountains or the sea? We cannot be in two places at once. We settle for a path that attracts us, turning our back on all others. In no time we have walked ourselves back into Contentment, albeit with a new sense of purpose. To be in Contentment may be the most satisfying and productive room of all. In the words of Bengt Lindstrom, who has worked with this model for years, "In Contentment we harvest the fruits of the seeds planted in Renewal. We ought to make the seasons of Renewal and Contentment last as long as we can. We cannot avoid Denial and Confusion, but we can make them less fearful."

2. Let the Four Rooms Work for You

There you have the story we tell ourselves. None of this do we say in meetings. However, one way we manage our own anxiety is to introduce people at the start to the possibility that things may not go smoothly all the time. We use a much leaner tale to describe what people might experience, referring them to the chart presented earlier.

For example, in Contentment (we tell the group), we're happy with the status quo and don't need to change anything. However, stuff happens. When struck by turbulent circumstances, such as information we'd rather not have, Denial is a normal retreat, a room to pass through but not live in. (If you confront people in Denial, they will deny it.) When we acknowledge that we don't like where we are, we move ourselves into Confusion. This is the room of uncertainty and high anxiety. It is also the room of possibility, for we now are looking full-time for a way out. As we confront the mess and confusion, we begin to see patterns not visible before. As we move toward creative solutions, we find ourselves in the Renewal Room.

We point out that people in this meeting could live in any room at any moment. We have known groups to move quickly from room to room as they deal with a sea of information. We also are not surprised that groups spend time in Denial and Confusion before moving into Renewal and Contentment.

Nor are we shocked when, on rare occasions, people freeze in place for what seems like an eternity. We tell people we are not predicting what they will do or requiring that they do anything. We're describing what could happen. We know that people would prefer that we, as leaders, keep everybody in Contentment or Renewal. Alas, we say, we don't know how to do that! We accept all the rooms as possibilities when you do purposeful work. We end our briefing with the hope that group members will do the same. Over the years, we have repeatedly heard people refer to the four rooms during a meeting, making legitimate their feelings, especially when things get rough. This structure makes things easier for everybody and helps us keep ourselves centered.

3. Experience the Benefits of Confusion

Now, here is what we do not say. Based on decades of experience, we believe that the Confusion Room, the décor of which is high anxiety, provides the most useful space in which to work when Renewal is your goal. In Contentment nobody needs to do anything. In Denial nobody wants to do anything. The apathy and lack of energy debilitates people. In Confusion everybody wants out. That is the place where leadership can make a big difference. Nobody likes Confusion, but in the middle of a tense meeting Confusion is not a bad place to be. Why would we consider it functional to live in a space no one likes? A physical/emotional state that some people take drugs to relieve? Well, we are not talking about clinical anxiety, that unfocused, nameless dread that overcomes many of us now and then and a few of us all of the time. We are talking about commonplace anxious meetings in a diverse world of nonstop change, when people wonder whether they will agree on a goal, be heard, solve the problem, make the decision, fashion the plan, cooperate, learn, and still make it home for dinner. In short, the Confusion Room has many doors. One leads back to Denial. The others welcome you to Renewal. Anxiety represents energy looking for a constructive outlet.

TEN WAYS TO MANAGE ANXIETY

There are simple ways to manage both a group's anxiety and your own. None require special training. All, however, take self-knowledge, patience, and the capacity to contain your feelings without acting them out. In short meetings of a day or less, a group may go in and out of the Confusion Room in minutes or hours. During meetings of 2 or 3 days, we are not surprised when people say they are confused for an extended period. It may not be much clock time, but it feels like a lifetime when you lead the meeting!

We base our coping strategies on the premise that a group will convert meeting-induced anxiety into excitement if you are patient. We offer you 10 ways to do that. When you feel secure using one, certify yourself as competent, and move to the next. After adding six of the 10 to your repertoire, give yourself a Certificate of Completion in Basic Anxiety Management (CCBAM). Or send us an e-mail saying what you did, and we'll award you one.

1. Use the Four Rooms of Change in Meetings

You need only 2 or 3 minutes to introduce this concept at the start of a meeting. When people know that you accept everything and everyone, they are more likely to accept everything and everybody, too. Hearing that you don't know how to avoid denial and confusion—indeed, that you consider both as normal—makes it easier for others to do the same. Moreover, you no longer need to worry about either state. Over the past decades, we have heard people say dozens of times, "Guess we've been in denial about that until now." Or, "I'm living in the Confusion Room." Such insights made public go a long way toward keeping groups whole. If they stay whole, they keep working.

2. Just Stand There and . . . Breathe

A natural tendency when anxious is to hold your breath. We may do that any time we are faced with stressful problems, difficult people, or intractable conflicts. Holding the breath increases the stress. Your palms sweat, muscles tense, and you feel jumpy or nauseous. Breathing relieves a lot. Taking two or three deep breaths is a helpful way to lessen the symptoms. There will be a moment in the near future where you have to make a decision and have no idea what to do. Here's something to try:

- Just stand there. Contain your feelings.

- Be aware of your agitation, your fear that things are getting out of hand, your impulse to fix it fast.

- Wait. Look around.

- Exhale as much air as you can.

- Take a big, deep breath.

- Hold it a few seconds.

- Repeat as needed, until somebody says what needs saying.

Try it. You'll be amazed at what you can do by exchanging the CO_2 in your lungs for oxygen. It's the greatest source of free energy on planet Earth. Be sure to tank up the next time you become anxious.

3. Check Your Negative Predictions

Negative predictions are often the cause of a great deal of anxiety. These are thoughts not of what's really happening but of what could go wrong. You jump into the future, thinking, "This is going to fall apart," "I can't pull it off," "The group is going to blame me," or "I'm going to fail." You feel as bad as if your prediction had already come true. While the scenario isn't real, the feelings are.

What to do? First, check your own thoughts. Are you making a negative prediction? If yes, pull yourself back by thinking, "It hasn't happened yet." Group members may have similar apprehensions. You have the advantage of knowing that if you wait, stay engaged, and keep alert, the situation will clarify. We believe the best way to approach such situations is with curiosity. What will this group do? Remember, you can always act, change direction, or call a break. The fact that you wait 30 seconds does not limit your options. You'll feel relieved, and the group won't even notice.

4. Track Your Inner Dialogue

To follow our own streams of consciousness while leading meetings is to explore an underground river so vast it is a wonder how we navigate it. It's amazing how often we fall into mind reading, imagining others' motives and attitudes.

What about that woman who's working her Palm Pilot under the table? Why did she come? Maybe she doesn't want to be here. I could ask her. But that might embarrass her. Maybe nobody wants to be here. I've heard that people in this place [profession, industry, age group] don't have much patience. They just want solutions fast. I'll never meet their expectations. What do they really want? If I knew, could I supply it?

Our inner dialogue never stops. We worry that we're moving too fast or too slow. We wonder what the quiet people think. We worry about having too much information or not enough. We wonder if we *really* have the right people, given what they are saying and doing. If a group could hear played over a loudspeaker what goes through our heads as we lead them, they might be vastly entertained. They would be unlikely to do any work.

Of course, ours is not the only inner dialogue. Add one for every person in the room. Consider it normal. Contain your anxiety. Recognize it, accept it, and consider it part of your job. Are you reacting to something in the room, or just what's in your head? Give yourself a reality check. Stay open to possibilities.

5. Experiment with Silence

In our facilitation workshops, we sometimes ask people to stand up, close their eyes, and imagine leading a group. We have them say out loud, "Does anyone have anything to add?" Their imaginary group says nothing. They are to stand in silence, eyes closed, and to raise a hand when they feel they must say something. In every group the first hand goes up in about 6 seconds. In 20 seconds, a quarter of the group have raised their hands. About 90 percent of hands go up within a minute. A few people, however, will stand mute until their legs buckle. If you are among them, you can skip this practice tip.

If you are not, here's your homework for your next meeting. When a group falls silent, pause and notice the moment you feel you must speak. Could you just stand there quietly and wait for 20, 30, 40 seconds more? Of course you couldn't. Thirty seconds is two lifetimes. But you don't have to endure such agony. Just try holding your tongue while counting slowly to 10. It will seem like an hour. However, you will do no damage to the group. You might, just might, leave enough space for someone to say something that could change everything.

Fortunately, somebody in every meeting knows what to say. You can only learn that if you wait long enough for them to say it. (If you try it, let us know what happens.) We keep the door open by listening without acting. We are mindful that each time we break the silence, we deprive someone of a chance to make a valuable observation. If we treat silence as a problem to be solved, we deprive others of a chance to take care of themselves. Just waiting often is all a group needs from us to shift toward active dialogue, reality checking, and creative collaboration.

6. Get People Moving

Nothing relieves anxiety better than physical movement. When people want to run from the task, that's the perfect time to invite them to get up—and keep working. In large-group meetings, we look for opportunities to let people move. It is natural for people to move when breaking into small groups. We ask people to post their own flipcharts. We solicit their help in taking notes, leading conversations, summarizing what they hear. It is natural for people to move if they need a break. We suggest that people who need a break take it at any time. They need not wait until midmorning or midafternoon. (If your mind is on personal needs, you can't focus on the agenda, anyway.)

When a meeting offers places for people to walk outside, we may ask a group if they want to take a longer lunch or take a short walk during afternoon break. We know of colleagues who combine movement with work by asking people to pair up, take a walk outside the room, and talk over an issue of concern to the group.

7. State the Obvious

The legendary Gestalt therapist Frederick S. Perls once stopped suddenly during a public lecture after several provocative comments. "Right now," he said, "I have nothing to communicate." He fell silent. There was a long pause, filled, said the meeting transcript, by "uneasy, random laughter." Perls (1957) waited several seconds. "Now," he said at last, "you see what I just did was a typical little piece of Gestalt therapy. I just expressed what I felt, and through this expression I managed to go on. I reestablished contact. I felt a warm laughter. I felt that you were with me at this moment. I was able to finish this unpleasant situation, this bit of discomfort that I and maybe you felt, when I became silent."

When you state the obvious, you signal your presence. You take care of yourself. Here are some phrases we have used over the years:

- "There are many opinions on this. Do we have them all?"

- "We've spent a long time on this topic. Is there more to say, or can we move on?"

- "I don't know about you, but I'm ready for a break."

- "Clearly, this issue stirs up strong feelings."

- "I'm confused about how this conversation relates to our purpose."

- "At this moment I haven't the foggiest idea what to do."

Anytime you state the obvious, wait 5 or 10 seconds for a reaction.

8. Consult the Group

Now and then we find ourselves leading groups with no idea what is going on and no idea what to do. Our strategy in these situations is to just wait. Nearly always somebody knows what to do. When nobody knows what to do, including us, we use our best tool of all. We stop meetings that are going nowhere and ask people what they want to do. Fortunately, we make this move rarely. It's reassuring to know we can do it, though. Try this in your next meeting when nothing is happening. Just say, "Hold it. We don't have to keep doing this." Then go around and ask each person who wants to speak to say whether he or she wishes to continue the meeting.

9. Grow Yourself by Listening to What You'd Rather Not Hear

In each meeting, we seek to stretch our capacity for tolerating statements we don't believe, ideas we oppose, and interaction styles that make us cringe. We stay aware of our internal tug of war between our own and others' concepts of right and wrong, truth and falsity, valid information, and what ordinary words mean. As we experience our potential for negative predictions, mind reading, stereotyping, mistrust, and anxiety, we find it easier to accept that this is where groups usually start.

The more we learn to live with uncertainty and remain curious about what's to come, the better prepared we are to value each group's struggle. So we resist the tendency to manage our own anxiety by talking, asking questions, explaining, repeating, or changing the subject. When we're not sure what to do, we don't do anything.

The more we learn to hear all views without reacting, the more a group is likely to express all sides of polarized issues. We train ourselves to listen for the parts of each statement with which we agree. We counteract our tendency to make a case (inside our heads, of course) for the parts we oppose. To the extent we act congruent with our philosophy that all statements contain value, the easier we make it for task groups to do the same.

10. Know Why You Are There

One way we manage our own anxiety is to remind ourselves before every meeting that what we are doing matters. We believe that we live our values in every meeting and find we need to align ourselves with the goals. What larger purposes are served by our presence? So much is going on during a meeting, we need to anchor ourselves in the meaning of this gathering if we are to know when to stand still and when to act. Larry Dressler put this issue eloquently while reading a draft of this chapter: "I spend quiet time before every meeting asking myself, 'What am I here to contribute? What are the central ideas on which I don't compromise?' If I know my 'center' in these matters, I can easily access it when I'm standing in the fire of anxiety, conflict, and confusion."

After some particularly tough moments leading a meeting, our colleague Grace Potts summed up her experience with anxiety in the form of advice to herself:

- "Process is more important than content.

- "Don't get distracted with last-minute panic attacks. I was so sucked into the panic over disruptive people, I missed a gaping error in the agenda. There was no time planned for moving from small groups back into the large group. It took sacrificing a break and some negotiating to end on time and finish everything.

- "Repeat the goals. Repeat the goals. Repeat the goals.

- "Repeat the ground rules. Repeat the ground rules. Repeat the ground rules.

- "You're really not in control of anything."

How did the meeting come out, Grace?

"All in all, it was excellent. We ended on time and met all our goals for the day. We even met a few goals we didn't know we had."

Principle 7: In Summary
....

Learn to accept anxiety as an inevitable traveling companion when the stakes are high, issues complicated, perceptions diverse, and answers uncertain. You can grow your capacity for leadership by increasing your tolerance for such natural conditions as disorder, ambiguity, and uncertainty.

Suggestions for Your Next Meeting

To make friends with anxiety, try one or more of these:

- Present the four rooms of change on a flipchart at the start.

- When things get sticky, consciously take two or three deep breaths. Notice whether you are making a negative prediction. If so, come back to the present.

- Look for a chance to stand in silence for 10 or 15 seconds, and see whether anybody fills it.

- Arrange for people to move if they've been sitting for a long time.

- If unsure of what to do next, try consulting the group.

Get Used to Projections

We all go to the same different meeting together!
—JIM MASELKO, consultant and trainer

When you are leading a meeting, do you get agitated with people who say nothing? Or with those who won't shut up? If someone expresses anger, do you become angry? Do you sometimes suspect that people are telling you what you want to hear? Or silently judging you on criteria never made explicit? Do you sometimes decide this group is "resistant," another group "ready to work"? Have you ever found yourself disliking, mistrusting, or ignoring somebody before you knew anything about that person? Or found yourself liking a complete stranger at first sight?

In each of these scenarios, you are caught up in the experience of projection. You attribute to things and people "out there" qualities that originate in you. Whether they have any basis in fact is irrelevant when you are projecting. Put on a uniform or clerical collar and people relate differently to you than if you were in shorts and a T-shirt. That's projection. Or notice what happens inside yourself the next time a leader stands up in front of a group and says, "My name is so-and-so, and I'll be running this meeting." Whether you decide to resist or cooperate depends largely on what you project on that person's looks, demeanor, and tone of voice.

We see, hear, or sense in others what our own psyches wish for us to see, hear, or sense, apart from any motive or intrinsic qualities in them. When we project on other people, we find in them clues that remind us of parts of ourselves. These could be parts that we detest or deny, or parts that we like very much.

This much of the concept of projection is widely known in a post-Freudian age. At the same time, we often remain unconscious of the projecting we do. Nor do we realize the extent to which others project on us, especially when we assume leadership. We grow up believing that others "make" us feel one way or another and that we do the same to them.

—EXAMPLE—

"You Remind Me of My Sister . . ."

Sandra was leading a meeting when she noticed a participant in the back making faces. Her first thought was "She makes me very uncomfortable. What is she going to complain about?" As the meeting went on, the woman seemed to have nothing but disapproval written on her face. During the next break, the woman approached. "Uh-oh," Sandra thought, "here it comes!"

"I just have to tell you this," the woman said. "You look a lot like my sister. I don't like my sister. So don't take it personally!"

EXPERIENCING YOUR PROJECTIONS

Taking it personally is, in fact, a big risk for most of us. In this chapter, we want to push you beyond the *concept* of projection to the *experience* of it in everyday living. How often, for example, do you look at a group and imagine that this will be an easy meeting or a hard one? How often do you decide just by looking that you need to be wary of certain people? We will show you ways to articulate your projections and to stay aware of the ones that come your way. Then we will suggest how you can use this awareness to increase your effectiveness in leading meetings. You may discover capabilities you never knew you had.

While projection is best experienced in "real time" with other people, you can begin studying the phenomenon alone. We have two methods that will bring you new insights and practical applications.

Method 1: Visit Your Internal "Four Rooms of Change"

Claes Janssen (2005), the Swedish social psychologist, whose work we described in Principle 7, created a short quiz that will help you invoke the world of your own projections. Answer each question yes or no:

1. Has it generally been difficult for you to identify with groups? Have you felt, for example, that somehow you did not mix, or that you had a different way of looking at things?

   _____ Yes   _____ No

2. Do you think you find it harder than most people to accept coercion and constraint?

   _____ Yes   _____ No

3. Do you have difficulty seeing yourself as a normal, well-adjusted person in the present society?

_____ Yes   _____ No

4. If you were asked what your life is about, what the strongest motive for you has been (whether you have made it clear to yourself or not), could you answer something like a search for truth or a search for freedom and a heightened sense of existence?

_____ Yes   _____ No

Now, regardless of your answers, reflect on people who would answer these questions no and those who would answer them yes. In the spaces here, write the most negative and most positive adjectives you can think of for both yes and no answerers.

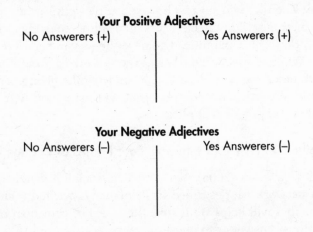

Your Positive Adjectives

No Answerers (+)   Yes Answerers (+)

Your Negative Adjectives

No Answerers (–)   Yes Answerers (–)

Compare Your Answers to These   We have found in workshops around the world that the lists come out much the same. For no answerers, people write positive adjectives like *confident*, *secure*, and *dependable*, and negative ones like *rigid*, *unfeeling*, and *authoritarian*. People describe yes answerers as *creative*, *visionary*, and *independent*, and also *lonely*, *out-of-touch*, and *anxious*. How many similar words do you have?

Here you have projection in action. The adjectives describe traits that you value in yourself (+), and traits that you deny or deplore (–). We all have these traits and countless others, some of which we know and some that we hide from ourselves. Anytime we label other people, we are projecting parts of ourselves.

Now overlay these adjectives on Claes Janssen's four rooms of change (see Principle 7). You get a matrix that looks like this:

Contentment (No +)	**Renewal (Yes +)**
Confident	Creative
Secure	Visionary
Dependable	Independent
Etc.	Etc.
Denial (No –)	**Confusion (Yes –)**
Rigid	Lonely
Unfeeling	Out-of-touch
Authoritarian	Anxious
Etc.	Etc.

Every room is fraught with projections, both positive and negative. When you lead a meeting, it's all there inside you and coming at you from all over the room. Any actions you take may trigger unexpected consequences. One of us once asked a person to hold a question until it could be dealt with together with other questions all at once. During the break, the person, seething with anger, approached and said, "What kind of facilitator are you? You have no right to put me off and make me wait!" We thought we were providing structure and order. She had herself being disrespected.

Even positive projections from others have pitfalls. When people see in you parts of themselves they admire, they set you up as a paragon you can never become. Inevitably, they find the clay feet under your shiny new shoes. Anybody who draws more (+) adjectives of praise from a group than they have reason to expect should not be shocked when the (–) list kicks in.

"What you just said has totally upset my worldview! I will never see things the same way again," said a young woman after we had given a brief talk. Later, she said she was confused and not finding the answers she hoped to get. We had become responsible for her enlightenment and had let her down—or so we projected!

Method 2: Find Your Many Parts If You Want to Lead Diverse Groups

Now comes the tricky part. To keep your projections from leading you to act unskillfully, own as many of them as you can. By "owning," we mean experiencing yourself with awareness, accepting traits that you don't like along with the ones that you do. The payoffs are many if you take the time:

- You will be less likely to reject or idealize others.

- You become less judgmental.

- You free yourself from having to be perfect.

- You contain anxiety when people say things you'd rather not hear.

- You experience fewer threats to your ego.

- You increase the range of people you can work with and not act out inappropriate feelings.

- You may learn at long last how to live that facile advice, "Don't take it personally!"

We learned to own our projections from the late John Weir, who with his wife Joyce helped thousands of people to self-discovery in their "Self-Differentiation" workshops (Weir, 1975).

How We Form "Percepts" from Projections   From the Weirs we learned how we turn the evidence of our senses into stories we create to satisfy whatever worldviews we have internalized. Our senses provide the factual information. Our brains turn sensory evidence (sights, sounds, smells, etc.) into personal perceptions ("percepts"), each one of which is unique. Every external stimulus sends an instant message to the brain, which compares the new sensation with those stored in memory. Our brains then form an image to reinterpret the experience in a way that satisfies us. Every experience we have from "out there" we turn into a percept "in here." We tell ourselves a story and act as if it is true.

We form percepts selectively, John maintained, in pursuit of an elusive unconscious goal: maximizing pleasure and avoiding pain. What constitutes pain and pleasure for you is wholly personal. You turn pure sensory experience into a story only you can tell by applying your unique "filters"—such as genes, family, culture, ethnicity, education, religion, gender, age, values, dreams, health, and so on. That is how some people, for example, come to perceive a group as "energetic, animated, and eager," while others see the same meeting as "out of control."

Change Your Percepts, Change Your Life   Now, here is the payoff if you lead meetings that matter. The more parts of yourself you discover, the greater the range of human behavior you will recognize and accept. Each time you find a new part, you increase your flexibility in handling new situations. Anytime you become upset with a group, you are experiencing some part of yourself worth investigating. Every single interaction you have carries in it the seeds for self-discovery.

Speaking "Percept Language"   Fortunately, there is a way you can accelerate this process. What follows may seem odd at first and perhaps off the point. If you stay with it, however, you may gain insights that cannot be gotten any other way. (If you have more insights than you need, you can always skip this.)

The Weirs created a language you can use to own your projections, meaning to get them at the gut level and not just as "interesting." Theirs is a linguistic variation on English that John named "Percept language" in contrast to "Object language," the grammar of everyday speech.

In Object language you externalize experience. Things keep happening *to* you. In Percept language *you* cause all of your own experience. Instead of generalizing and abstracting, you speak concretely, specifically, and descriptively. No matter what happens "out there," what happens inside you is your own doing. Thus, in this linguistic system, you "do" yourself through your perceptions.

In Object language, you think (to yourself, if you are the leader), "I'm bored silly with all the stupid questions." In Percept language, you think, *"I bore myself* with the stupid question *part-of-me."* In Object language, you say, "This group is out of control." In Percept, you say, "I have the group-in-me be the out-of-control *part-of-me."*

If you persist with this grammar, you may experience with great clarity how you create your internal projection screen as you lead a meeting. Each time you internalize a part of you previously experienced as beyond your control, you free yourself a tiny bit from an unconscious, self-imposed limitation. You will never again be "hooked" by that trait in other people. Years ago in meetings we became keenly aware of our extreme irritation at people who insisted that everything be perfect and go smoothly all the time. Reflecting on this, we came to see that this was exactly the pressure we placed on ourselves. We were projecting our perfectionism on people just like us and disliking them for it. When we stopped projecting, we gave up needing to be perfect. And we became more patient with those who still did.

Rules of Grammar: Percept 101   You can learn basic Percept grammar in four easy lessons.

1. Change *it*, *this*, and *that* to *I* and *me*. Make *yourself* the source of every thought, feeling, and action.

Object Language	Percept Language
"It doesn't matter."	"I don't matter."
"That makes sense."	"I make sense."

2. Change passive verbs to active. Make yourself the key actor.

Object Language	Percept Language
"I'm bored."	"I bore me."
"That's exciting."	"I excite me."

3. To each noun or pronoun, add the phrase "in-me" or "part-of-me."

Object Language	Percept Language
"You're frustrating me."	"I frustrate myself with the you-in-me."
"He makes my life fun."	"I make my life fun with the him-in-me."

4. Give up (for the moment) "I think," "I feel," or "I see" in favor of the phrase "I have ＿＿ be ＿＿."

Object Language	Percept Language
"I think she's fabulous."	"I have the her-in-me be a fabulous part-of-me."
"I see the group is in confusion."	"I have the group-in-me be a confused part-of-me."

Watch Your (Percept) Language!   We need to emphasize that Percept is not intended for everyday speech. Most people would think you odd indeed if you began talking in a restaurant about the "waiter-in-me" or in a seminar about the "lecture-part-of-me." Percept language's purpose is to aid you in your own growth. You use it to refine your perceptions and temper your judgments when you lead meetings.

To this end, you can *think* in Percept whenever you choose. We value our ability to translate ourselves as we work with groups. We hear people's judgments as "parts of the them-in-us" rather than objective comments about how the world is. We quite literally make ourselves aware that each time somebody says something, we are hearing the way that person (in us) puts the world (in him or her) together.

PARTICIPANT: I'm frustrated by all this repetition.

Us (silently translating): I have the her-in-me being in the frustrated part-of-her. (She is speaking about her experience, not making an objective statement.)

We translate our own quick judgments about "them" into parts of us, clues to our own projections, rather than objective qualities of other people. We learn more about us and become more tolerant of others.

—EXAMPLE—

"Let's Get These People Back to Reality!"

We're leading a strategic planning meeting. People are trying out new ideas. "I think we should tear the building down and start from scratch." Another says, "Not nearly enough. I say sell it and move across the river." A third chimes in, "Let's get real here. The most we can afford is a new paint job and a public relations campaign!"

As leaders, we form unspoken judgments: "silly ideas," "too flighty," "not creative enough," "futile reasoning," and so on. We are thinking in Object language. We could easily panic and accept that it's our job to get people thinking "realistically" (e.g., the way *we* think).

Instead, we pause. In our heads each of us does a little dance: "I have the group-in-me be a silly *part-of-me* . . . a too flighty *part-of-me* . . . an uncreative *part-of-me* . . . a futile *part-of-me*." Within seconds we awaken ourselves to the judgments we make and what awesome responsibilies we take on. Thus, we free ourselves to find out what *they* think they are doing. We hear people doing themselves. Every idea is a part-of-them. Our job is to help get enough of the parts out so they can have the whole range to work with. Rather than slow them down or cut them short, we honor all the parts, in ourselves and in them.

> LEADER: "Let's keep the ideas coming until we have a spectrum of possibilities."

Of course, you might say that without knowing Percept language. Now, you have another way to describe what you do!

Percepting Your Experience   Here we provide some tips for helping you connect with the percept part-of-you.

1. You choose your own judgments, fears, and fantasies. Nobody does anything to you. You "do" yourself. You may be tempted, for example, to imagine some group members are "undermining" your agenda. In the world of percept, you undermine yourself with the group-in-you.

2. You are unlikely to convince others that their truths are wrong and yours right. Hear others' statements of "fact," "truth," and "reality" as percept parts-of-them (the them-in-you!).

3. Reduce any tendency you may have to blame others for what you do or feel.

If you can do yourself as these tips suggest, you are less likely to take "it" personally. Next time somebody says something you take as critical of you, say (silently to yourself), "I criticize me with the [name of person]-in-me." In other words, recognize that you do the reacting, you call it criticism, you experience the guilt, and you generate the feelings. The other person becomes an image on your "percept screen."

Practicing Percept Language   Translate these sentences from Object to Percept language:

Object Language	Percept Language
a. She's a friendly person.	I have her be _____ _____.
b. This group annoys me.	I annoy myself with _____ _____.
c. You are very smart.	I have the _____ be a _____.
d. That was awesome!	I have that be an _____ _____.

Answers:
a. I have her be the friendly part-of-me.
b. I annoy myself with the group-in-me.
c. I have the you-in-me be a very smart part-of-me.
d. I have that be an awesome part-of-me.

Principle 8: In Summary
....

Projection means experiencing as originating "out there" parts of ourselves that we like or reject. We may project our hopes and fears on others, making them responsible for our feelings and our fate. Others do the same to us, especially when we take leadership. There are many benefits to becoming aware of your projections. Not least of these is learning to detach enough from what happens in meetings that you stop taking personally whatever people say or do.

Suggestions for Your Next Meeting

- List the positive and negative parts of yourself that you became aware of as you read this chapter. How can you use this awareness in the next meeting you lead?

- In the last conversation you had, can you identify any part of you that you projected onto the other person(s)?

- Write a sentence in everyday language describing how you feel about Percept language.

  Right now, I _____.

Now, translate your sentence into Percept language. (Use active verbs, change *it* to *I*, and locate all of the action inside you.)

  Percept language: I [active verb] _____
  myself with the _____
  part-of-me.

- Now, describe somebody you know well in everyday language.

  I think that [person's name] is _____,
  _____, and _____.

  Next, translate your description into percept language.

  I have the [person's name] _____
  in-me be the [list of traits] _____
  parts-of-me.

(If you'd like feedback on your solutions, send us an e-mail at fsn@futuresearch.net.)

Be a Dependable Authority

If you can keep your head when all about you
Are losing theirs and blaming it on you,
If you can trust yourself when all men doubt you
But make allowance for their doubting too,
If you can wait and not be tired by waiting,
Or being lied about, don't deal in lies,
Or being hated, don't give way to hating
And yet don't look too good, nor talk too wise.

—RUDYARD KIPLING, "If" (1895)

Kipling's poem contains three more stanzas, 15 "ifs" in all. He ends by saying that if you can do all these things "you'll be a man, my son." We like his poem because Kipling vividly describes to his child exactly the challenges every meeting leader faces. Anytime you assume authority, people test your dependability. The more emotional the agenda, the tougher the testing. It is your job to keep your head, not take things personally, be patient and not too full of yourself. The pay-off comes when you learn to trust steadfastly that when you hang in long enough, no matter how disquieting the agenda, you will be doing the best you can.

Anybody can be an authoritarian. We learn that behavior in infancy. Later on, schools, churches, the armed services—any place where discipline prevails—reinforce us. Rare is the person who grows up untouched by a demanding authority figure. No wonder we struggle to bridge the vast gap between authoritarianism and legitimate authority.

In this chapter, we will help you learn to be a dependable authority. The more you immerse yourself in authority dynamics—the universal experience of leaders and the led—the easier it will be for you to avoid trapping yourself with your own power. In the previous chapter, we dissected the role projection plays in everyday life. Here we turn our lens on handling the projections you face as a leader. The key skills we advocate are

- recognizing authority projections when they come at you;

- staying alert to ways you stimulate authority projections;

- deflecting authority projections;

- keeping your own projections in check;

- responding appropriately.

UNDERSTANDING AUTHORITY DYNAMICS

As leader, facilitator, or content expert, you assume a position of authority. Like it or not, you draw projections. How you use your authority affects a group's performance. We believe that breakthroughs—in communications, problem solving, and decision making—come with real-time shifts in the way people interact in meetings. These shifts are more likely if you manage your role dependably. We know well the temptation to please by doing for people what they can do for themselves. Or to treat every suggestion as a problem we must solve. Above all, we have had to unlearn our tendency to take group frustration personally and withdraw or clamp down when things get sticky.

We work hard to sit on our own wishes to control uncertainty, minimize conflict, squash differences, and keep everybody happy. We have learned to contain our own fantasies that this group will fly apart if we don't keep the lid on. We have come to accept our internal tug of war between common sense and our need to be all-knowing and beloved. From years of dissecting our own experiences, we have learned to trust that out of chaos people inevitably find order. It's our job to protect the conditions for discovery. We reinforce our functional authority by making sure that for a chosen goal the right people are present and have enough time for the task. We maintain credibility by hearing from all who want to speak, getting a spectrum of views out before moving toward action. We let people be responsible for their decisions. When the decisions are ours, we act without apology.

EVERYONE REACTS TO AUTHORITY

If you choose this path, start by appreciating just how deep is every group's relationship to authority. From the beginning of time, people have brought authority projections to meetings and shined them like a laser beam on whoever was in charge. You may have yourself be a nice person—likable, easygoing, and all that. Or maybe you see yourself as brisk, businesslike, and a little proud that you are so hard to please. Regardless of what positions you take in meetings, no matter how strict or loose your meeting management, whether you are the boss, a staff person, or an outside consultant, you can assume some people will struggle with you in predictable ways.

In Percept language, they confront—without being conscious of it—whatever past experiences with authority the "you-in-them" stirs up. In new groups, this phenomenon is a certainty. In existing groups, you can count on it anytime new people join the group. You also will find projections stimulated any time a group's equilibrium is upset.

Our knee-jerk projections on authority often stem from long-ago transactions with parents, grandparents, siblings, friends, and teachers. We come into the world helpless and dependent. As infants we flip between an "all good" or "all bad" state of mind. A baby can turn from happy giggles one minute to screaming fury the next. It becomes an adult's lot to appreciate and/or fix the situation.

Not until the second decade of life do most of us learn to hold onto opposites. Along the way, we may experience the positive influence of trustworthy adults and learn grim lessons from those who misuse authority. One coping skill adults develop is the ability to recognize the "both/and" nature of things. We have the capability to know that good and awful coexist in us. Unfortunately, we don't always use that knowledge well.

It may come as no surprise that participants in new groups unknowingly externalize past authority struggles into tugs of war with whoever leads them. Even groups of grown-ups start out in a primitive state. However, groups can mature very quickly if you let them. A mature working group recognizes and uses its own authority. It accepts your leadership without blindly trusting or mistrusting you. Whether a group gets to that point depends on how you handle their authority projections. If you accept that the biggest hook for them is your role, not you, you can learn to avoid stimulating either dependency or rebellion.

EXPERIENCING AUTHORITY PROJECTIONS

New groups seek to find out how much you know, how much authority you assume, and how you intend to use it. Groups typically begin by complying. They act eager to please you. One school of thought holds that a large, unconscious subgroup hopes that you have the magical power to make everything all right. That's fantasy, of course, and eventually, when the work becomes difficult, the group will disillusion itself.

Others, who came in hating authority, may have you be their enemy and, in extreme cases, seize on the slightest opportunity to defy you. Nobody, you included, knows who are which, until somebody takes you on and several others sit back to enjoy the show.

All this, of course, is theoretical. But, then, consult your experience. How often have you led a group where some people will follow you into the fire and others throw cold water on anything you say? We call the first way of relating to authority "dependency" and the second "counterdependency."

LEADER: We'll take a 10-minute break.

DEPENDENT GROUP: Great, your timing is perfect!

COUNTERDEPENDENT GROUP: Ten minutes isn't enough!

RECOGNIZING DEPENDENCY

Don't confuse dependent behavior with cooperation. While you may bask in the warmth of groups that do whatever you ask, be aware that they may end up doing nothing for themselves. If you enjoy taking more and more on yourself, the advice that follows is not for you. If you would like to avoid or drop the Big Parent role, you need to (a) reduce the demands you make on yourself and (b) get dependent groups to accept their responsibilities. Dependency is based on wishful thinking rather than reality. You can spot the telltale signs when people (a) tell you what they think you want to hear, (b) check in with you every time before acting, and/ or (c) defend you, and the rules, against criticism. Anytime you find yourself working harder than anyone else in the meeting, you foster dependency. Is that what you want?

Here are common dependency signals:

They idealize you (You are a hero/heroine who does no wrong.)

> "If you say so, who am I to argue?"

> "You have a way of seeing things that nobody else does."

> "I envy your style, the way you handled _____!"

They seduce you (Surely you enjoy being charmed!)

> "You're a very kind, sensitive person."

> "You look like you need a [hug, back rub, cup of hot tea]."

> "I can't thank you enough for what you are doing for us."

They curry favor (Don't you need a new best friend?)

> "I'll move the flipcharts. You have better things to do."

> "I know you like baseball. I've got an extra ticket for Saturday."

> "I clipped an article that reinforces the point you made yesterday. Would you like me to give it out to the group?"

This behavior harms no one so long as you don't crave it and reinforce it. If you come to expect it as your due, and if you miss it when you don't get it, you're hooked. You're a fish in play, a dependency junkie, and no longer in charge of yourself. You may find yourself going out of your way to elicit praise and avoid tension, soothing to the ego, bad for the task.

RECOGNIZING COUNTERDEPENDENCY

You won't feel so benign when groups react against your authority. You may experience counterdependency as mistrust, cynicism, or boredom, none of which you signed up for. Telltale signs are (a) countering everything you say, (b) avoiding eye contact with you, and/or (c) verbally attacking you. Here are some clues to watch for:

They undermine you. (I know better and can prove it.)

"X has a theory that clearly refutes yours."

"Evidently you haven't seen the latest research on that."

"Been there, done that. Show us something new!"

They devalue you. (You are incompetent.)

"You don't have enough experience to be leading us."

"You're not listening to anything we say."

"You are forcing your agenda down our throats."

*They mount a verbal attack.** (You are a threat to the group.)

"You have manipulated us."

"You are undermining our work."

"If you stay, we go."

---

*We are describing situations where you are not in physical danger. If you ever feel that a member might physically hurt you or someone else, get help!

HOW YOU ATTRACT AUTHORITY PROJECTIONS

The behaviors we describe here have more to do with your authority role than your personality. Anybody who takes charge risks projections. How you react to these projections determines whether they slide harmlessly by or entangle you in a mire of fight and/or flight from the task. Alas, you too have feelings! When group members project on you for better or worse, you may use your own past experiences with authority to hook yourself into regressive behavior.

Indeed, you can easily make things worse by turning the spotlight on yourself. Not only is the group off-task when it starts focusing on you. The minute you're hooked by whatever was said, you risk leaving the task, too. At that point you are no longer leading the group. You have joined them!

Ask yourself these questions to see how a group's dependency might lead you to lose sight of the task:

- Do you love attention and believe the high praise?

- Do you want to keep a group happy all the time?

- Do you crave positive feedback?

Or:

- Do you feel turned off by their transparent "phoniness"?

- Do you want to knock some sense into their silly heads?

- Are you impatient with how long it takes them to learn?

Next, notice your feelings when people devalue or attack you:

- Do you feel like a failure?

- Do you want to justify yourself?
- Do you panic and shut down?
- Do you want to strike back, harder?
- Do you want to run and hide?

HANDLING AUTHORITY DYNAMICS

However you respond to these questions, we want to iterate some useful advice you probably have heard a dozen times:

Don't take it (the "them-in-you") personally!

When people project on you, you can choose to interpret their remarks as saying more about them than you. They are doing the "you-in-them." If you have a hard time depersonalizing extravagant praise and/or devastating criticism, we have a few tips for staying out of trouble.

1. Respond Briefly to Dependency

Be aware that early in the life of any group, people may unconsciously deny their responsibility for learning, deciding, or acting. They will look to you to meet their needs. Be empathetic. You've been there, too. You need not withhold positive responses. Just don't overreact and reinforce gratuitous feedback.

GROUP: Are we doing it right?
LEADER: (Nods approvingly—no detailed performance reviews)

GROUP: How do we compare with other groups?
LEADER: You're doing fine. (Rather than gushing, "You did more in the last hour than any group I ever worked with!")

GROUP MEMBER: You are terrific the way you look so calm in the midst of all this confusion.

LEADER: Thanks. (Do not add, "I certainly don't feel that way inside!")

To be a dependable authority in the face of dependency is to accept others' feelings as natural, support people, and avoid making the issue bigger. The fewer words the better.

2. Get a Subgroup for Counterdependency

Counterdependency is a little trickier. Sometimes a single person expresses a feeling that others might consider risky to own. When people want to fight you because you're in charge, you would do well to pause before doing anything. This is the perfect moment to just stand there. If you need an anxiety reliever, take a deep breath.

We have a long list of things we work on *not* doing while just breathing. It includes explaining what the point is, rolling our eyes, showing irritation, wisecracking, pushing back, and/or ignoring the person by going on to somebody else. While standing there, we remind ourselves that our goal now is keep the group from splitting and losing sight of its task. To do that, we seek to open ourselves to the validity of the speaker's point—that is, to find the "speaker-in-us." Whatever impulses we have, we do our best to contain them. Our only action step is clear: find that person an ally (the process described in detail in Principle 6).

MEMBER: I'm not getting anything out of this. What's the point?

LEADER: Anyone else have questions about what we're doing?

Our advice to you is to legitimize the questioning and let the group handle this. If some people wonder about the point, others will supply it. If nobody sees the point, then open the conversation to everybody. Whatever you do, avoid escalating the authority projection! Don't tell people what they should get or what they ought to experience.

When you add your point of view, be direct about what you hope to do. Then ask how well you are succeeding.

3. Deflect Direct Attacks

And now, the toughest situation of all. What can you do when people question your competence and/or attack your legitimacy? We find it hard to generalize advice without specific instances. Sometimes people may be on to something. In that case, you had best own up.

> MEMBER: You just don't get it, do you?
> LEADER: You may be right. Anyone else thinking I don't get it? (If no one responds we might say, "Are there others here who don't get it?")

> MEMBER: You don't have enough experience to be working with us.
> LEADER: I haven't been in exactly this situation before. I'm willing to stay with it if you are.

> MEMBER: You're not listening to anything we say.
> LEADER: Perhaps I missed something. Tell me again.

> MEMBER: You are trying to force your agenda down our throats.
> LEADER: Yes, I have an agenda. But if you feel like it's being forced down your throat, let's step back. Anyone else have concerns about the agenda?

If you lead enough meetings, there will come a day when someone cannot contain his or her negative authority projection on you. The hook is too big, too compelling, and too tempting to ignore. This person may have been building to this moment for a long time. Whenever we ask a group of colleagues if they have ever been attacked verbally, most say yes. Often it happened only once, but they never forgot the moment. So prepare yourself, and practice subgrouping.

—EXAMPLE—
"You Manipulated Us!"

Our memorable moment came in the last hour of a productive strategic planning session. There were 60 staffers for a large agency dealing with finance throughout the Americas. As the action plans were applauded, one participant said directly to us, "You may think you have done a good job, but actually all you did was manipulate us into dreaming up unrealistic scenarios and making plans that will never be implemented. You just set everybody up for disappointment!"

> GROUP: (Stunned silence)
> LEADERS: (Open-mouthed)

This statement, said with great feeling, challenged everything we believe. First, it shocked the group. Everyone waited for endless seconds to see what would happen. He certainly took us by surprise. We had to work hard to keep from lashing back. In our heads, we were hooked.

What a destructive comment! Where was he the last 3 days? Maybe he's right, for indeed we have helped groups make plans they could not carry out. Not this time. Now we had the whole system in the room. These action plans were endorsed by top executives and board members. This was not about us. The organization's credibility was on the line. Could he get the group off the action plans and on to him? Would they suddenly see their commitment and creativity as artifacts of clever facilitation techniques, with no chance of being implemented? Were we just the "manipulative part of the us-in-him"? A big projection screen for his own disappointments?

All of this—process and content—we imagined while just standing there. If you have come this far with us, you can see what we considered the key issue, philosophically, theoretically, and practically. This person had put himself at risk for becoming the group scapegoat. The success that most people were experiencing could easily be blunted if they rejected him. The question to ask at this point was not "Anyone else feel manipulated?" Rather, the question was "Does anyone else have concerns about carrying out the action plans?"

In this instance, we never got to ask it.

One person said, "Well, I committed to taking these actions, and I intend to follow through." Another said, "It's true we have made unrealistic plans in the past. But not this time." Several nodded agreement. As we just stood there, wonder of wonders, an ally jumped in. "We agreed here at the start that all ideas are valid," said a senior executive. "He's entitled to his opinion, and we should respect it." The moment for scapegoating passed. One top leader got up and reiterated his support for the plans, reassuring the skeptic that he intended to see them carried out.

BECOMING A DEPENDABLE AUTHORITY

Defiant group members often take shots at the leader. You are there to be shot at and will be. It's no fun, but it's no big deal, either. If you don't fall dead and you don't shoot back, you will have a quick truce, followed by a peace treaty.

Principle 9: In Summary
....

Anytime you assume authority, people test your dependability. The more emotional the agenda, the tougher the testing. Being dependable means staying cognizant of authority dynamics as they play out in every group. You cannot avoid authority projections. They come at you anytime you lead. You can learn to keep your head and not take things personally. You can respond appropriately to dependency and counterdependency without becoming hooked on your own brilliance or undermined by your suspected shortcomings.

Suggestions for Your Next Meeting

- Tell yourself silently that you are doing the best you can every minute, no matter what happens. Give yourself a break.

- Become self-aware when you bark orders, judge comments, use sarcasm, roll your eyes, talk too much, repeat yourself, cut people off, rush to finish, and/or [add your own worst habit]. Pick a habit, drop it just once, and see what happens.

- Identify for yourself, without acting on it, one projection that you are making on others. Recognize one projection that comes from the group toward you. Let it go by if you can.

Learn to Say No If You Want Yes to Mean Something

You got to know when to hold 'em, know when to fold 'em,
Know when to walk away and know when to run.

—KENNY ROGERS, "The Gambler"

When Ronald Reagan was president of the United States, his wife became famous leading an antidrug campaign under the slogan "Just Say No!" In fact, saying no is not an easy sell. People who live in a 24/7/365 world of can-do and must-do ascribe negative traits to anyone who uses the world's shortest negative. No is a sign of hostility; it implies passive-aggressive impulses; it brands the speaker a defeatist; it undermines creativity, goodwill, and good humor. For many managers, consultants, facilitators, and staffers, saying no can be interpreted as cowardice, disloyalty, or even sabotage.

In this chapter, we speak to several audiences: department heads, supervisors, or managers who feel pressure from somebody higher up to do something they doubt will work; consultants external and internal who are under the gun to deliver extraordinary results under questionable conditions; staff people in finance, information technology, engineering, and human resources who imagine their jobs are on the line anytime they are tempted to negotiate conditions for success; teachers, health care professionals, and civil servants who are constantly in the public eye.

Many conscientious souls are addicted to saying yes when every synapse in their bodies screams "no way."

Few people will deny leaders something they want badly. Some people in authority expect that they can buy transformational meetings like copy paper. If a meeting requires 3 days, get it down to 2; if you need 2, try 1. That's it. "Faster/shorter/cheaper" may be the 21st century's corporate mantra, invoked on all occasions whether practical or not. Managers and staff people feel compelled to accept every challenge, and consultants, in the enthusiasm for new contracts, are prone to set their own expectations higher than reality will bear.

Paradoxically, this does not lead to fewer meetings. Faster and shorter often means more frequent, less conclusive meetings with costly unintended long-term consequences.

—EXAMPLE—
Excluding Key Corporate Staffers

We were once invited to help a manufacturing plant with strategic planning. We learned very quickly of considerable conflict between the plant and corporate office. To our surprise, the plant manager refused to involve any-one from the manufacturing hierarchy in his planning meeting. We had several talks with him about involving these others. We pointed out the opportunity to reduce the conflict and increase the plant's influence over policy decisions.

Nevertheless, the plant manager held firm. He was risking too much in bringing corporate staffers he con-sidered adversarial to his plant. We thought he was wrong to imagine that the plant's problems could be resolved internally when the plant depended on policies it disliked.

Eventually, we gave up and declined this assign-ment, realizing that to accept meant colluding with the plant manager's wish to defer the conflict rather than deal with it. Under the conditions laid down, we be-lieved there was no way he could get what he wanted. He was setting his staff up for disappointment.

THE COSTS OF SAYING YES WHEN YOU'D RATHER NOT

Well, first let's review the benefits. If you are on some-body's payroll, you (perhaps) get to keep your job. If you are an external consultant, you add some days to your cal-endar. Against these considerations—not trivial if you have mouths to feed—are the costs to your professional integrity, to an organization that trusts your judgment, and to your feelings of self-worth. You have little to gain on any of these criteria by going into projects that have failure written all over them.

As outside consultants, saying no to doubtful work keeps us available for worthy projects we can do with en-thusiasm. (Unless you say no, the good work will always materialize when you are least able to do it—usually the day after you said yes to a doubtful proposition.)

WHEN TO SAY NO

How do you tell somebody who "needs" a miracle that you don't think it's in the cards given their limitations? Have you ever said yes and lived to regret it? We suggest that in the long run, you are better off turning down activities that you think will fail. In a world where progress is eked out one meeting at a time, our definition of "failure" is the mirror image of success. People meet and learn nothing new, do nothing after the meeting that they have not done before, and—worst case—become more cynical and frustrated.

There is a saying that the definition of insanity is doing what you've always done and expecting different results. In the spirit of common sense, we advise that when you are faced with a request to get transformational results under the same old conditions (wrong people in the room, too little time, unrealistic objectives, etc.), try doing something different yourself. Don't pretend that you can deliver under those circumstances.

—EXAMPLE—

Changing Yes to No in an Impossible Situation

"I've walked out on hopeless projects," said a West Coast colleague of ours. "The most traumatic one was a non-profit agency whose job was to bring technology to nonprofit groups. I agreed to help with convening their national partners; then I found out that the new director was at war with all of her partners. Her behavior was abusive and directive, and she wasn't giving me any flexibility. Every design idea I would suggest, she'd reject. She was basically trying to dictate what I should do. I realized I could not help her. I told her, 'I can't do it this way, I'm sorry, but we have two completely different styles.' I had a couple of sleepless nights, but thank goodness I didn't go further."

Here are more scenarios where no might help more than yes.

1. **Logistical.** The deadline is too tight, and the resources can't be found in the time allotted. "When do you want the outcomes?" the potentially responsible party asks; "Yesterday," says the impatient person in authority, and everyone laughs. That is the opening line for a negotiation you may regret.

2. **Existential.** The request exceeds the design limits of human capability. You are asked to lead a process to provide an innovative vision, comprehensive plan, and implementation strategy for the next 5 years with a board of directors that has only a day to meet and three key people have to leave early.

3. **Pragmatic.** You believe that high participation leads to successful implementation and are asked to get hundreds or thousands of others in an organization or community to commit to plans that they had no hand in shaping.

4. **Self-protective.** You accept responsibility without having authority. The person in charge has delegated to you the merger of two departments, neither of which reports to you. High cooperation and rapid action are required. You could do it if you had enough clout. You don't.

5. **Value laden.** The objective contradicts a deeply held value of yours. You are asked to run a meeting where the people in authority may not support the outcomes. You believe they are using the forum to manipulate compliance.

6. **Realistic.** You are convinced that the person asking your help has imposed conditions almost sure to set up a failure. They intend, for example, to exclude key people who might oppose the plans being made,

or they want a decision accepted without allowing people enough time to work through the implications.

7. **Expediency over all.** You are asked to shave the quality of your service to produce results "faster, shorter, and cheaper" than whatever time frames and costs you have quoted.

8. **Just plain wrong!** This last reason for saying no is obvious: when you believe that the request would make you an accessory to acts you consider immoral, unethical, or illegal. This scenario may sound extreme to you, but we read examples in the newspaper every day.

Say No with Alternatives

Your no need not come in the form of a flat-out refusal. Rather, if you get a request that seems shaky, you can offer to talk about it. Perhaps the parties involved don't realize what's involved in what they are asking. Perhaps they underestimate the challenge. Perhaps they have no experience with the limits they have imposed.

—EXAMPLE—
A New City Transportation Plan

A local transportation department head asked us to manage a large-group meeting to create a resident-based funding strategy for his city's new traffic management plan. A small team of managers and experts had created the plan during months of intense meetings with no community input. While the request was legitimate, we could not in good conscience run a meeting to get people to fund a plan they had not seen before. If the city was willing to treat the plan as a draft proposal, open to community influence, we could design a meeting to accomplish three goals at once: a new plan supported by everybody—managers, experts, and citizens; an implementation plan that included funding strategies; and high commitment to act by the key actors.

We said we understood the dilemma of changing course late in the process. Our conversation was a short one. To our surprise, the department leader called back 2 weeks later saying that he had concluded that citizen buy-in was important and agreed to present the plan as a work in progress to be shaped by all. That was a contract we could accept. The meeting ran, the plan was modified and funded, and despite tensions among competing interests (e.g., cyclists and motorists), it went into effect with much less hassle than if the original plan had been followed.

DON'T PROMISE MORE THAN YOU CAN DELIVER

Keep expectations realistic. This precept is your best insurance that yes will mean something. You're better off with low expectations and surprising results. Most of our no's take the form of "Here's what we can do under the conditions that you are proposing, and here's what we can't do."

—EXAMPLE—
Rethinking an Academic Mission and Curriculum

A university department chair wanted a 1-day retreat with 12 faculty members to clarify their mission and build a curriculum. The faculty was split about what kind of program to offer and admitted their meeting dynamics were dysfunctional. Our no sounded like this: "We can't help you accomplish those goals if you don't include others, such as students and alumni, in the discussion. You will not learn anything new from each other, you will miss perspectives that only students and alumni have, and you'll keep repeating old dynamic patterns.

"Here's what we realistically can do in 1 day: help you think about your issues in the context of trends in society that faculty are aware of, and identify your choices in planning for the future." We offered no guarantees that the group's unsatisfying dynamics would change, only that we would do our best. The meeting went better than we expected, in part because we had people explore "the whole elephant"—those external factors affecting the whole department rather than revisit relationships that were hard to change. One outcome was a decision to include students and alumni in a subsequent retreat.

Principle 10: In Summary
....

Saying no is an underused skill in a shorter-faster-cheaper society. If you say no to conditions where you are not likely to succeed, you will save yourself and others much time and effort in meetings. If you prepare yourself to say no, you will feel more secure, successful, and centered each time you say yes.

Suggestions for Your Next Meeting

Useful phrases to practice in private until they feel natural:

- "I wish I could do that. All my experience tells me that we need to modify the plan so that you'll get what you want."

- "That's a worthy goal. I'm not sure I know how to achieve it."

- "Maybe it would be best to wait and do this project when we can get the conditions for success lined up."

- "I'm not the right person for this. I [don't agree with the goal; question the legality; etc.]."

- "Under those conditions, I doubt I can succeed. Here's why."

- "No way. Find someone else to do your dirty work!" (You were planning to quit anyway.)

Ten Principles, Six Techniques: A Summary

This book contains many rules, guidelines, tips, procedures, practices, and techniques for leading meetings. Over the years, we have noticed ourselves using certain ones repeatedly. We believe that if you learn to make these six moves, you will be able to handle almost anything that comes up.

We urge you to consider these suggestions only in relation to our 10 principles. You'll have a much easier time with any of them when you make friends with anxiety, get used to projections, and see yourself as a dependable authority. You have little to gain using any of them if you don't have the right people in the room.

1. To quickly establish a sense of the whole, go around a group and have people say where they are (i.e., "differentiate") themselves. (Principle 3)

2. To keep meetings from fragmenting, find an ally for a person at risk by asking an "anyone else" question. (Principle 6)

3. To interrupt polarization, help people identify subgroups in conflict and dialogue among themselves. (Principle 6)

4. To stimulate creative ideas and broader participation, ask people to talk over a topic in small groups,

then report to everyone what was said. "Please talk with your neighbor [or in trios or quartets] for ___ minutes, and see what ideas you have." (Principle 4)

5. If stuck on what to do next, consult the group. Somebody always knows. (Principle 7)

6. Offer to end the meeting if people believe progress cannot be made. "We don't have to keep doing this. I'd like to hear from each of you whether you think it's worth continuing." (Principle 7)

Conclusion:
Changing the World
One Meeting at a Time

As we seek to live by the principles we have described, we feel healthier, more in charge of ourselves, and in a better position to make a difference in society. We conclude this book with an invitation to leaders everywhere. You have more chances than you realize to make positive ripples in the world. You can turn frustration and cynicism to creativity and energy on a daily basis. You needn't wait for a cataclysmic issue. The practices we describe apply equally to the thousands of ordinary meetings during which much of the world's work gets done. You can make a positive difference anytime you set it up so that people do things together that none can do alone.

A few years ago, Rolf Carriere, then a regional director of UNICEF, became concerned about improving education for Indonesian schoolchildren. He joined with government ministries in an ambitious plan to decentralize secondary schooling, bringing together stakeholders, including children, from across the country. "Considering how much time and resources we spend in meetings," he said at the start-up session, "it should shock us that we don't get more important work done. Meetings are where we confront and resolve the problems and issues society faces. If we cannot transform our ability to act in meetings, how can we expect transformation in society?"

Carriere's call to action led to 40 interactive meetings in communities around the country, a concerted effort that effectively decentralized responsibility for children's education. If people in a largely rural Southeast Asian nation are capable of such meetings, why not your staff, board, committee, task force, congregation, hospital, school, or business?

We offer you three incentives for experimenting with the principles we advocate. Our first is based on systems thinking. No matter how loosely you perceive the connection, everything is joined to everything else. Each meeting impacts, for better or worse, the larger systems of which it's a part. Each time you help people act constructively, you encourage positive ripples in the wider world.

Sharad Sapra, a medical doctor and UNICEF official, attended a Future Search in Bangladesh. Soon after that he ran conferences in Iran on the plight of battered women and of street children. He moved on to Africa and in November 1999 sponsored two conferences on the future of southern Sudanese children displaced by years of war. Stakeholders—including children, expatriates, tribal chiefs, teachers, and local officials—envisaged a Sudan 5 years later at peace. Not long after, Sharad asked us to train 50 Sudanese aid workers in our methods.

A week later several went into a Sudanese village that had recently been bombed and ran a conference aimed at the fate of child soldiers. Within months, thousands of young people under age 16 were demobilized and returned to their villages. In the next 5 years, several schools and clinics were built in the south; and in January 2005, the northern and southern Sudanese signed a peace treaty. "When we did the first Future Search," Sharad wrote, "we said 'PEACE 2005,' and everyone laughed at us. I think what we did was create hope in a hopeless situation, a dream in place of a daily life of suffering."*

*When this was written in 2007, the North and South remained at peace despite a desperate situation in the Darfur region of western Sudan.

Our second incentive is pragmatic. You're putting the time into meetings anyway. If you could add up the total hours people spend in meetings, calculate the cost using any formula you wish, and track the outcomes using any criteria you choose, you would be astounded at the unfavorable input/output ratio. After writing that sentence, we quickly found on the Internet a summary of meeting research proving not only that point but also a point we made earlier in this book: you can find data to prove anything. Here is a summary of the study of studies (Meade, 2006):

- Eleven million meetings occur in the United States every day.

- Most professionals attend 61.8 meetings a month.

- People report that over 50 percent of their meeting time is wasted.

Dick Haworth, chairman of Haworth, Inc., the global office furniture company, noted after bringing people from around the world to a Future Search, "We have got more done in the last 3 days than we ever did during months of traditional strategic planning, and we expect to implement a lot faster." Six months later, Haworth executives reported ripples from that meeting spreading throughout the company and around the world.

Our third incentive is personal. You will free yourself of considerable self-induced pressure as you learn to lead by observing more and judging less. You have a lot to gain by working with people the way you find them. You may discover that there are enormous untapped resources to be mobilized when people have a chance to bring all of themselves to every encounter. When a meeting generates positive, constructive energy, everybody does better work. If you long for meaning in daily life, one improbable place to find it is in the meetings you run. For us, as we live these principles, we find ourselves more secure, enthusiastic, curious, and open to new challenges, ready to walk down paths none have walked before.

Part of humanity's common heritage is the innate capability to cooperate. That is the antidote to the tendency, also innate, to separate over differences. That we spend so many hours in meetings without using our latent resource is a terrible waste. You need not perpetuate bad meetings. We hope we don't come across as grandiose in affirming that when meetings really matter, stacking the deck for success is existentially the right thing to do. If you share our conviction, you can change the world one meeting at a time.

Working some years ago with Auntie Malia Craver, a wise Hawaiian elder, we learned something that her ancestors had passed down for thousands of years. After listening to a half-hour presentation on how involving everyone in planning could improve community health, Auntie Malia said simply, "Oh, we have a word in our language for what you've been talking about. "

"What is it?"

"*Laulima*," she said.

"What does that mean?"

"It takes many hands together to do a task."

Bibliography

Ackoff, R. L. (1974). *Redesigning the future: A systems approach to societal problems*. New York: Wiley.

Agazarian, Yvonne M. (1997). *Systems-centered theory for groups*. New York: Guilford Press.

Agazarian, Yvonne M., & Sandra Janoff. (1993). Systems theory in small groups. In H. Kaplan & B. Sadock (Eds.), *Comprehensive textbook of group psychotherapy*. Baltimore: Williams & Wilkins.

Asch, Solomon. (1952). *Social psychology*. New York: Prentice Hall.

Auden, W. H. (1947). *The age of anxiety: A baroque ecologue*. New York: Random House.

Bion, Wilfred. (1961). *Experience in groups*. London: Tavistock.

Brown, Juanita, & David Isaacs. (2005). *World café*. Berrett-Koehler.

Bushe, Gervase R. (1995, Fall). Advances in appreciative inquiry as an organization development intervention. *Organization Development Journal, 13*(3), 14–22.

Buzan, Tony. (1991). *Use both sides of your brain: New mind-mapping techniques* (3rd ed.). New York: Plume Books.

Cresswell, Julie. (2006, December 17). How suite it isn't: A dearth of female bosses. *New York Times*, Business, 1, 9–10.

Emery, Fred E., & Eric L. Trist. (1973). *Toward a social ecology*. New York: Plenum.

Faucheux, Claude. (1984, October 10–13). Leadership, power and influence within social systems. Paper prepared for a "Symposium on the Functioning of the Executive," Case Western University, Cleveland, OH.

FutureSearching, the Newsletter of the Future Search Network. Available: www.futuresearch.net

Janssen, Claus. (2005). *The four rooms of change* (Förändringens fyra rum). Stockholm: Ander & Lindstrom. (An English version of the book is available online at www.claesjanssen.com/ books. For training in its use as a change management tool, see www.andolin.com/fourrooms.)

Lawrence, Paul R., & Jay W. Lorsch. (1967a, November–December). New management job: The integrator. *Harvard Business Review*.

Lawrence, Paul R., & Jay W. Lorsch. (1967b). *Organization and environment: Managing differentiation and integration*. Boston: Harvard Business School Press.

Lewin, Kurt. (1948). *Resolving social conflicts*. Edited by Gertrude W. Lewin. New York: Harper & Row.

Lewin, Kurt, Ronald Lippitt, & Ralph White. (1939). Patterns of aggressive behaviour in experimentally created "social climates." *Journal of Social Psychology, 10*, 271–99.

Lippitt, Lawrence L. (1998). *Preferred futuring: Envision the future you want and unleash the energy to get there*. San Francisco: Berrett-Koehler.

Madsen, Benedicte, & Søren Willert. (2006). *Working on boundaries: Gunnar Hjelholt and applied social psychology*. Aarhus, Denmark: Aarhus University Press.

Meade, Chris. (2006, October 1). Meeting research study summary. Available: www.studergroup.com/dotCMS/knowledge AssetDetail?inode=269049

Merrill, Alexandra. (1991). *Self-differentiation: A day with John and Joyce Weir* (three-video set). Philadelphia: Blue Sky Productions.

Mix, Philip J. (2006, September). A monumental legacy: The unique and unheralded contributions of John and Joyce Weir to the human development field. *Journal of Applied Behavioral Science, 42*(3), 276–99.

Owen, Harrison. (1997). *Open space technology: A user's guide*. San Francisco: Berrett-Koehler.

Perls, Frederick S. (1957, March 6). Finding self through gestalt therapy. Cooper Union Forum Lecture Series: *The Self*. Available: www.gestalt.org/self.htm

Rogelberg, S. G., D. J. Leach, P. B. Warr, & J. L. Burnfield. (2006). "Not another meeting!" Are meeting time demands related to employee well-being? *Journal of Applied Psychology, 91*(1), 83–96.

Schweitz, Rita, & Kim Martens (Eds.). (1995). *Future Search in school district change*. Lanham, MD: Rowman & Littlefield.

Weir, John. (1975). The personal growth laboratory. In K. Benne, L. P. Bradford, J. R. Gibb, & R. D. Lippitt (Eds.), *The laboratory method of changing and learning: Theory and application*. Palo Alto, CA: Science and Behavior Books.

Weisbord, Marvin R. (1987). *Productive workplaces: Organizing and managing for dignity, meaning and community*. Jossey-Bass, San Francisco.

Weisbord, Marvin R., & 35 Coauthors. (1992). *Discovering common ground*. San Francisco: Berrett-Koehler.

Weisbord, Marvin R. (2004). *Productive workplaces revisited: Dignity, meaning and community in the 21st century*. San Francisco: Jossey-Bass/Wiley.

Weisbord, Marvin, & Sandra Janoff. (2000). *Future Search: An action guide to finding common ground in organizations and communities* (2nd ed.). San Francisco: Berrett-Koehler.

Weisbord, Marvin, & Sandra Janoff. (2005). Faster, shorter, cheaper may be simple; it's never easy. *Journal of Applied Behavioral Science, 41*(1), 70–82.

Weisbord, Marvin, & Sandra Janoff. (2006). Clearing the air: The FAA's historic growth without gridlock conference. In B. Bunker & B. Alban (Eds.), *The handbook of large group methods: Creating systemic change in organizations and communities*. San Francisco: Jossey-Bass.

INDEX

About the Authors

Marvin Weisbord and Sandra Janoff have led meetings for decades all over the world. They codirect the Future Search Network, an international nonprofit dedicated to offering collaborative planning services in any language, any culture, for whatever people can afford. They are coauthors of *Future Search: An Action Guide* (2nd ed., 2000). They have trained more than 3,000 people in using their principles. They are members of the European Institute for Transnational Studies and the Organization Development Network.

Marvin Weisbord was a professional consultant with business firms and medical schools from 1969 to 1992. He is a fellow of the World Academy of Productivity Science and for 20 years was a partner in the firm Block Petrella Weisbord, Inc., and a member of NTL Institute for Applied Behavioral Science. He received a Lifetime Achievement Award in 2004 from the Organization Development Network, which voted his book *Productive Workplaces* (1987) among the five most influential books of the past 40 years. He also is author of *Organizational Diagnosis* (1978), *Discovering Common Ground* (1992), and *Productive Workplaces Revisited* (2004).

Sandra Janoff is a consultant and psychologist, and has worked with corporations, government agencies, and communities worldwide on issues of globalization, sustainability, and humane practices. She was a staff member in

Tavistock conferences sponsored by Temple University in Philadelphia and The Tavistock Institute of Human Relations in Oxford, England. She also has run training workshops in systems-oriented group dynamics. Sandra taught mathematics, physics, and chemistry from 1974 to 1984 in an experimental high school and ran workshops in Pennsylvania schools on alternative practices in education. She is coauthor with Yvonne Agazarian of "Systems Thinking and Small Groups" for the *Comprehensive Textbook of Group Psychotherapy*. Her research on the relationship between moral reasoning and legal education was a lead article in the *University of Minnesota Law Review*. Sandra has a Ph.D. in psychology from Temple University.

Contact the authors:
mweisbord@futuresearch.net
sjanoff@futuresearch.net

For workshops with the authors, see www.futuresearch .net or contact Future Search Network at fsn@future search.net, (800) 951-6333 or (215) 951-0328.

To join Future Search Network and help change the world one meeting at a time, go to www.futuresearch.net and click on "Membership."

ABOUT BERRETT-KOEHLER PUBLISHERS

Berrett-Koehler is an independent publisher dedicated to an ambitious mission: Creating a World that Works for All.

We believe that to truly create a better world, action is needed at all levels—individual, organizational, and societal. At the individual level, our publications help people align their lives with their values and with their aspirations for a better world. At the organizational level, our publications promote progressive leadership and management practices, socially responsible approaches to business, and humane and effective organizations. At the societal level, our publications advance social and economic justice, shared prosperity, sustainability, and new solutions to national and global issues.

A major theme of our publications is "Opening Up New Space." They challenge conventional thinking, introduce new ideas, and foster positive change. Their common quest is changing the underlying beliefs, mindsets, institutions, and structures that keep generating the same cycles of problems, no matter who our leaders are or what improvement programs we adopt.

We strive to practice what we preach—to operate our publishing company in line with the ideas in our books. At the core of our approach is *stewardship*, which we define as a deep sense of responsibility to administer the company for the benefit of all of our "stakeholder" groups: authors, customers, employees, investors, service providers, and the communities and environment around us.

We are grateful to the thousands of readers, authors, and other friends of the company who consider themselves to be part of the "BK Community." We hope that you, too, will join us in our mission.

BE CONNECTED

Visit Our Website

Go to www.bkconnection.com to read exclusive previews and excerpts of new books, find detailed information on all Berrett-Koehler titles and authors, browse subject-area libraries of books, and get special discounts.

Subscribe to Our Free E-Newsletter

Be the first to hear about new publications, special discount offers, exclusive articles, news about bestsellers, and more! Get on the list for our free e-newsletter by going to www.bkconnection.com.

Get Quantity Discounts

Berrett-Koehler books are available at quantity discounts for orders of ten or more copies. Please call us toll-free at (800) 929-2929 or email us at bkp.orders@aidcvt.com.

Host a Reading Group

For tips on how to form and carry on a book reading group in your workplace or community, see our website at www.bkconnection.com.

Join the BK Community

Thousands of readers of our books have become part of the "BK Community" by participating in events featuring our authors, reviewing draft manuscripts of forthcoming books, spreading the word about their favorite books, and supporting our publishing program in other ways. If you would like to join the BK Community, please contact us at bkcommunity@bkpub.com.